IN HASTE FROM TIBET

In Haste from TIBET

RINCHEN DAKPA
AND
B. A. ROOKE

ROBERT HALE · LONDON

© Rinchen Dakpa and B. A. Rooke 1971
First published in Great Britain 1971

ISBN 0 7091 2259 4

Robert Hale & Company
63 Old Brompton Road
London S.W.7

PRINTED IN GREAT BRITAIN BY
CLARKE, DOBLE AND BRENDON LTD
PLYMOUTH

CONTENTS

ILLUSTRATIONS

ILLUSTRATIONS

PICTURE CREDITS

Numbers 1, 2, 3, 4, 9, 10, 14, 15 were provided by Paul Popper Ltd. All other pictures were provided by the authors.

INTRODUCTION

WHEN I was twelve years old, I had to escape, with my uncle, to India, in a hasty flight from the Red Chinese, who have invaded my country, Tibet.

This is the story of that escape and of my first twelve years of boyhood in Tibet. It is a plain tale, told as I remember it. I have no family to whom I could refer for dates and data. The result is a boy's eye view of life in Tibet between 1947, when I was born, and 1959 when I arrived in Assam.

As a child in Tibet I was unaware of the tragic changes taking place in my country, but of course I have since learnt that the Red Chinese army crossed our eastern frontier in October 1950. The Tibetan army resisted strongly, but they were hopelessly outnumbered and inadequately armed and it was not long before news reached our capital city of Lhasa indicating all too clearly that our country would soon be overrun by the communists.

All our appeals for outside assistance failed, and by the time I arrived in Lhasa from my country home in Western Tibet in 1954 the Red Chinese were established in the capital, although our government was still ostensibly in office. The Chinese pretence of 'liberation', providing us only with 'guidance and assistance', was still being maintained outwardly and our Government's struggles against their unreasonable edicts and demands were not in general known to (or noticed by) the Tibetan man in the street. To me, a 7-year-old boy in Lhasa for the first time, everything seemed quite normal.

Although I lived with my uncle, a Tsedrung monk official with a government appointment, I was too young to pay any attention to political difficulties and am not aware that any were discussed in the house.

Shortly after my arrival in Lhasa my uncle became engaged in work at Norbulingka, the Dalai Lama's summer palace. With the exception of feast and ceremony days, he no longer had to attend the Pota-la daily with the result that, as far as I know, he did not have very much contact with the Red Chinese officials.

He was very strict with me, insisting that I concentrate on my studies and I rarely took part in the daily life and festivals of Lhasa. There had always been a number of Chinese residents in the town, and, although their numbers were now swollen by the invaders, it never occurred to me to question their presence.

After I had been in Lhasa about three years, my uncle was appointed by His Holiness the Dalai Lama to be Governor of Kongpo Province and in 1957 we moved to Tsela Dzong, the governor's residence in South-eastern Tibet.

Tibet is a vast country, roughly equivalent in area to Western Europe. It is a land set virtually in the sky, with limitless plateaux, towering mountains, thunderous waterfalls and tranquil lakes. A tropical sun shines brilliantly in azure skies, but a sudden thunderstorm can literally rattle the house and shatter the glass in the windows.

Lhasa, the capital city, is built on a plain a mere 12,000 ft above sea level, but some of the snow-filled mountain passes heave up to 20,000 ft and the plateaux are swept bare by screaming ice-laden winds. Yet peaches and cherries grow in wild profusion in Kongpo, Drekung valleys are splattered with buttercups and daises, enormous roses bloom in the gardens of the houses in Lhasa and the entire land is enveloped in an immutable tranquility. A land of indescribable beauty where one could absorb, almost touch, the gossamer of Infinity. A land that neither I, nor any other free Tibetan, can ever replace in our hearts.

There were one or two cars and jeeps in Lhasa, but outside the city roads were few and undeveloped. The Chinese lost no time in building one road from Lhasa to their eastern border to carry their trucks and soldiers, but travel was still mainly across country on horseback.

Communications too were almost non-existent. There were no telephones or morning posts; official mail was sent by human 'runner', or if it was very urgent by 'pony express', and could take anything from one week to three months, depending on the destination.

In such circumstances, it is hardly surprising that the determined Tibetan resistance to the invaders that continued in Eastern Tibet and the growing hostility farther West, affected me not at all—until in 1959 the Tibetans openly revolted and the fighting spread. Then suddenly we had to run for our lives across the Himalayas into Assam.

So it happens that the reader will find few allusions to political or ceremonial life in Tibet. But these aspects of our life have been written about by scholars, older and better qualified than I.

Nevertheless, I hope the reader will find some interest and entertainment in the life story of a boy who lived on 'The Roof of the World'.

"THE CHINESE ARE COMING!"

KONGPO is a large fertile province in south-eastern Tibet. It is known throughout the country for the excellence of its walnuts and wood, peaches and pork; a province of great beauty, it is the 'Garden of Tibet'. In springtime the countryside is ablaze with wild peach and cherry blossom; in summer pigs and cattle feed on the peaches too numerous to gather and peach-fed pork is exported to Lhasa.

A ridge of high mountains thrust eastwards from the west to halt in a grassy 18,000-foot spur (nicknamed the Sleeping Elephant because of its contours) wedged into the course of the Tsangpo and compelling the river to fork south-west, leaving a tributary, the Nyangchu, to flow north. Thus the two rivers almost encircle the foot of the spur like a fast-flowing moat.

Set almost at the top of this headland stood Tsela Dzong, an imposing fortress built of massive weathered stone. This was the official residence of the governor of the province. Enclosed within the tall stone walls were the government offices, the prison and courtroom, stables, storehouses and the official and private quarters of the governor's household and staff.

From its high perch on the shoulder of the mountain, the Dzong watched over the many villages dotting the plain, which ranged away to the feet of the mountains spearing the sky on the far horizon.

Below Tsela Dzong, about 12 miles north across the plain beyond the Nyangchu, there was a Chinese barracks. Chinese officers frequently came to the Tsong for meetings with my uncle. They always brought an escort of twenty or thirty soldiers with them, all of whom seemed to me to be very young, many of them apparently only about 15 years old.

To the South, across the Tsangpo, there was a Tibetan barracks with Khamba soldiers. They too came for meetings, sometimes alone but more often with the Chinese.

It was after my uncle had been Governor of Kongpo for two years that the Chinese policy in Tibet suddenly began to be noticeably tougher; the Tibetans revolted and the fighting spread.

It was March, 1959 and I was just 12 years old.

It was very late in the night. There was no moon. Everyone in Tsela Dzong had been asleep for some hours.

The sound of hammering on a distant door beat in my head. I tossed in my sleep in an effort to shut out the noise.

My brother came suddenly into the room and shook me awake.

"Get dressed quickly! The Chinese are coming!" he told me abruptly and left.

Half-sleeping, I jumped out of bed into the pitch darkness and began groping round for my clothes. My room was as dark as a blackboard. I had no lamp; electricity had not yet reached beyond our capital city of Lhasa.

I started to dress hurriedly, fumbling into my shirt and chuba, feeling about for the boots I could not see. I could tell from the noise about the Dzong that everyone had rushed up on hearing the peasant's shouts of warning.

Listening to the hurried footsteps and low anxious voices outside my room, I finished dressing, sat on my bed and waited. No one came, so at last I went into the passage to look for my brother. He was much older than I and I hoped he would tell me what I should do next. By the light of the lamps now lit in the corridors I could see everyone running urgently to and fro, very busy packing up as much as they could. No one had time to notice me!

I wandered about uncertainly. As a matter of fact I was still not sure what all the busy rushing was about; I only remembered that in my sleep my brother had told me to get dressed quickly.

At last I saw him and followed him back and forth until he finally told me to go to the stables and saddle my pony myself. It was evidently everybody for himself.

I made my way down the stairs, beginning to feel a little frightened by the tension and bustle all round me. Everyone was saying the Chinese were very near our Tzong and our lives could be in danger. I became much more afraid on hearing this and ran quickly across the courtyard, past the already loaded mules and into the stables, just as the last horse was saddled and led out.

The stables were blind dark. Hurriedly I groped round for my saddle and slung it across my pony. By this time everyone was outside and ready to leave, I could hear the horses beginning to move off across the courtyard.

I fumbled desperately in the dark with the unaccustomed task of getting my pony ready as panic began to mount in me that I would be left behind. My pony, sensing my fearful urgency, was restless and impatient, throwing her head, snorting and jittering about her stall. This didn't help me. But at last I was ready. Just in time to join the cavalcade!

There was no moon, the night was impenetrable as we rode off at a gallop. I heard the Tsela Dzong dogs barking as we sped through the castle gates. We could see nothing; we just had to ride and hope for the best.

I had no idea which direction we were taking, I had to let my pony go its own way and wonder how all the horses could possibly keep charging along through such darkness. It was like dashing through black velvet.

We galloped headlong down the mountain in silence. We were not allowed to talk for fear the Chinese might be close by. The whippy mountain grass helped to muffle the thunder of the horses' pounding hooves.

Once I heard my brother cough. He sounded nearby but I could not see him—I could not even see my pony's head! My uncle decided to break away and cross the river to the Tibetan Khamba Barracks. The rest of us rushed on through the night.

At last, after racing along for what seemed to me to be hours, I heard a dog barking in the distance and knew we must be nearing a village.

The barking grew louder as we reined in our horses to trot through the village, finally pulling up in front of a large house surrounded by a high wall.

One of the servants dismounted and knocked loudly on the stout outer door. Nobody answered, but a dog barked furiously from somewhere behind the wall. The servant knocked several times, but still the only answer was the dog barking. We realized that the people must be afraid to answer thinking we were the Chinese.

We all began shouting that we were not Chinese but members of Tsela Dzong. Eventually a servant opened the courtyard door a very little and cautiously looked out. Seeing at once that we were indeed Tibetans he smiled with relief and opened the door wide for us to ride into the courtyard.

As soon as we entered the house the owner and his family greeted us warmly, in spite of being dragged from their beds in the middle of the night, and tea and food was at once prepared for us.

To my complete astonishment, when I came to get down from my pony I discovered that my saddle had slipped away during our runaway ride and was lost. To this day I have no idea how this could have happened without my knowing. In my haste in the darkness I must have forgotten to tie the saddle girth securely, but I was too rushed and anxious to have noticed. The saddle had evidently slipped off as we galloped helter-skelter through the night and gone it was! There was nothing to be done! I joined the others for the meal now put before us.

All the family joined us—including the children, who had all woken up with the noise of our arrival. They were quite puzzled as to who we were and what we were doing there so late in the night eating and drinking as though it was the middle of the day!

I was much too tired to eat anything, but courtesy required that I should sit with everyone until the meal was over. My head felt as heavy as a solid pot of gold; no matter how I tried not to fall asleep, my eyes kept closing and my head fell forward onto my chest. I tried many times to hold it up as I should but I was not successful and felt very pleased when at last everyone had finished their tea and conversation and my brother pulled me up by my arm to lead me off to bed. I went to sleep at once, not caring what sort of room or bed I slept in, nor where the Chinese might be.

Very early next morning my brother woke me and told me I must go out and look for my saddle before having my breakfast. It was certainly a very beautiful saddle, made of wood like all Tibetan saddles; as it was carved from a fine piece of Kongpo walnut inlaid with turquoise and trimmed with silver, it was reasonable that I should be told to look for it. I set off through the village, riding my pony bareback, both of us still feeling very tired from the long night ride. But luckily I did not have to search for very long. My saddle was lying by the side of the road at the entrance to the village. Feeling very relieved, I picked it up and rode happily back to the house. On my return, my brother and his companions just laughed at me as I hungrily sat down to my breakfast.

Later that morning our host sent a servant back to Tsela Dzong to see if the Chinese were really there. On his return, the man reported he had seen no sign of them and we decided that the peasant's warning the previous night must have been a false alarm. The servant told us that my uncle had returned to the Dzong with some Tibetan soldiers but so far everything was peaceful. Nevertheless, it was decided it would be unwise to go back until we could learn something more definite about the situation.

In recent months the Chinese attitude in Tibet had hardened. We had been hearing of villages destroyed and monasteries looted. Children were being taken from their parents and sent away to communist schools in China. In the smaller districts of Kongpo Province they had now taken to checking up on everything very closely, demanding more and more food from the farmers to feed the ever-increasing numbers of Chinese soldiers. Their attitude changed from one of civility and cajolery to aggressive bullying and fierce retribution for any defiance. This caused many Tibetans to revise their own attitude of tolerance and passive resistance. Now, as the invaders began to enforce their will on the people, the Tibetans reacted angrily and began to strike back.

As battles commenced, Tsela Dzong was an inviting objective for the Chinese. Strategically placed—guarded by the mountains ranging westwards behind its back, standing high on the hillside with an uninterrupted view to the north, east and south across the immense fertile, populated plain, with the Tsangpo and the Nyangchu looped protectively round the foot of its mountain. A stronghold and a 'watch tower' the invaders would covet at once in the new situation. Also, the Chinese would make every effort to arrest my uncle. As Konchi of the Province he would be a great prize; the capture of His Holiness the Dalai Lama's Representative for the Province would have a dispiriting, if not demoralizing effect upon the rebelling people.

With all this in the balance, it was decided, after much thought, that my brother and the servants should return to Tsela Dzong whilst it was still peaceful to pack up some of the things we had left behind in our rush the night before. It was settled that as soon as my brother returned, accompanied by my uncle, we would be wise to continue our flight. Meanwhile I was to stay behind in this house with one of our servants until they got back.

I felt a bit lonely, being left in a strange house where I knew no one; but on the other hand I was very pleased to be rid of the lessons which I had to study every day at Tsela Dzong!

The servant left behind with me soon went off to have some chang (Tibetan beer) and I stayed in my room with nothing to do.

I was sitting on my bed, wondering how to pass the time, when two of my host's children came and stood just inside the doorway watching me very seriously. I could see they were trying to become my companions but were too shy to ask. We looked at each other solemnly for several minutes, then they began to giggle and shuffle about but continued to stand in the doorway.

I felt as shy and awkward as they did. In the six years since I had left my parents' home I had had little chance to mix or play with other children and I had no idea where to begin. Positions were sharply defined in Tibet and my uncle's official status and strict regime placed a good deal of reluctant isolation upon me. I had had no companions of my age at all at the Dzong, and now, confronted with these would-be playmates, I was completely at a loss!

At last, after a great deal of thought, I managed to tell them to come in, which they did at once very happily.

Now they stood by my bed giggling and smiling, whilst I looked at them again in silence, racking my brains for something to do or say. Then I noticed that one of the children was holding a doll in her hand and I asked her to show it to me. This she willingly did and the shyness was broken.

We all began to relax. Then we discovered our main difficulty was communication. I did not know enough Kongpo dialect to understand them—I had had no need or opportunity to speak it except for a few polite phrases of greeting—and the children could not speak Central Tibetan.

After several false starts, I discovered they could play Tibetan Chess, a popular game in Central Tibet, where it is called the King and the Soldiers. It is not unlike the English game of Fox and Hounds played with draughts. We have two Kings and twenty-four soldiers and the game is for the soldiers to capture the kings or vice versa. The children did not have the board and sets to play with, so I drew a sketch of the board on a piece of paper whilst the children went off to collect twenty-four small stones for the soldiers and two large ones for the Kings.

Then we settled down in my room to play and there was no need for conversation. The time passed very nicely.

After three days my brother returned from Tsela Dzong, bringing our horses and mules loaded with our personal possessions. My uncle was with him. He had decided that we must go to Lhasa to see His Holiness the Dalai Lama and join the other senior Government officers at Norbulingka.

It was a long way to Lhasa. News of hostilities and increasing activity by the Chinese army made the road from Nyitri to Lhasa sound perilous, it seemed wiser to take a more roundabout route across country. Some of the way we would have to go was high and difficult, with deep snow already almost blocking the mountain passes we must cross. It would take at least three weeks of steady riding.

Thinking of this our host begged us to stay on for a day or two to be rested and well prepared for the journey and my uncle gladly accepted the invitation.

The children came into my room once or twice hoping for a game of chess. I wanted to play with them very much, but my uncle had forbidden me to do so. I could not very well explain this to them and I am afraid they went away feeling puzzled and hurt, thinking I no longer wanted to be their companion. This made me very sad, but there was nothing to be done.

At the end of the week we set off on the long journey to Lhasa. We rode all day and spent the night at another Kongpo house. Here we were again invited to stay on for a few days and my uncle accepted.

Looking back now, it seems strange that we accepted these invitations after our precipitate departure from Tsela Dzong. I think the only possible explanation for our apparent dalliance must be that my uncle had official business to attend to and arrangements to make, about which, of course, I knew nothing.

At any rate, in spite of constant news of increasing Chinese troop movements and Tibetan guerilla activities, we stayed on in this house for several days.

2

PRAYERS FROM GREEN TREES

THE time passed slowly for me in this strange house. During the six years I had lived with my uncle I had been expected to conduct myself with scholarly dignity at all times and my life had been spent almost entirely in solitary study. Now, relieved of my Tibetan studies in our present haste away from Tsela Dzong, I found myself quite at a loss to know what to do during this week's halt.

Talk of increasing Chinese aggression and Tibetan resistance sharpened my anxiety for the safety of my parents at home in Bhakar, many days ride away. No-one told me what was going on, but I noticed many people that called on my uncle looking troubled and concerned. There was a general air of tension, a feeling of impending danger which nobody either could or would explain and I became increasingly bewildered and lonely.

In this mood I slipped away from the house, walking aimlessly through the hills, my thoughts at home with my family.

The sun was hot and orange in a turquoise sky; huge white woollen clouds chased each other into fantastic shapes, spurred along by a high clear cooling breeze. They seemed so near that I felt I had only to reach upwards to grasp a handful of the scudding white wool for myself.

A rabbit started up at my feet, its white tail pointing an erratic course as it sped down the hill, bobbing across a golden and bronze carpet of primulas. I walked on until I reached a small hillock, sheltered from the wind by a knot of silver birch trees. The green springy grass looked inviting and I lay down on my back to watch the cloud patterns designing themselves above me. A golden eagle soared silently across the sky, its vast wings resting on the wind that carried it swiftly into the distance. I wished I was a legendary boy who could ride perhaps on the back of such an eagle and visit my parents in Bhakar; but alas, if wishes were horses (or eagles!) then all beggars would ride!

I closed my eyes and listened to the wind sighing through the trees, showered with a cascade of notes from a skylark overhead.

I felt relaxed, drowsy and very homesick.

At home my father and his neighbours would all be busy with the springtime ploughing. From dawn to well after dusk he would be walking behind the wooden plough guiding the steel-tipped share in straight cutting lines as the yak and dzo pulled it steadily forward.

My home was a farm in Bhakar, a village in Drekung, a province in Central Tibet. Here I was born in the Year of the Fire Hog (1947) and lived with my parents and younger brother. Also living with us were my grandparents, my father's brother and his wife and four servants. Our house, like most Tibetan houses, was white. It was shaped like an L on its back. The main gate led into a roofed courtyard which was lit by a large unglazed skylight in the centre. Round the courtyard were the stables and beyond these the storerooms, which formed the ground floor of the building. The house itself was on the first floor overlooking the courtyard. It had a flat parapet roof with large prayer flags at each corner linked together by strings of smaller flags. The corner flags flew from slim trees which were renewed every New Year's Day, when we put up fresh prayer flags. When the trees were first cut from the woods and erected at the four corners of the roof, they were green and leafy and had fluffy white blobs, like cotton wool, flowering all over them. They always looked very beautiful and festive in the winter snow and sunshine, with the new, gaily-coloured prayer flags fluttering round them. But soon the cotton balls blew away. At first we replaced them with imitation ones made from our own sheeps' wool, until gradually the leaves, too, dried and blew away, then the trees remained quite bare, except for the prayer flags, until we cut our fresh ones for the next New Year.

Bhakar, which means White Cow, consisted of four houses, including our own. My father was the headman of this village. It lay on a rise at the head of a broad valley, the houses snugly sheltered by towering mountains at their backs; acres of wheat, barley, rye and golden mustard spreading like a sea down the wide valley before them. Two of our neighbours were quite comfortably placed, with enough land and cattle to supply their needs, but the third family was quite poor. A widow with two children, she had only about twenty-five sheep and a few goats. Her son was about my own age and we were great friends.

Life at home was very peaceful and happy, although there was always a great deal to be done. As well as crops to see to, Father had a wide variety of livestock needing constant watchfulness and attention. Yaks can be aggressive and will fight to the death—not only over a dri (female yak) but in pitched battles with any intruding yaks unwise enough to stray from other herds—unless someone is at hand to separate the combatants. Eagles frequently stole the lambs; leopards, bears and wolves enjoyed a calf dinner if they could get one. We kept goats, not to eat, but for their hair, which is coarse and strong and good for making the sacks for storing grain.

Every morning my mother was up at first cock cry. There were no clocks or watches in our village; the moon, the stars and the cock's cries told us the season, the date and the time. Full moon was the fifteenth and the thirtieth of each month and the first cock cry announced the appearance of the Thorang-karchen (Dawn Star) with clockwork precision. Mother's first task, after she had washed and dressed herself very nicely, was to check that all the butter lamps on our altar had sufficient butter to keep them burning, for they must glimmer constantly and each lamp only contained enough butter to burn for twenty-four hours. Next the silver bowls must be filled to the brim with fresh water. These bowls were emptied and polished every afternoon and refilled with water every morning before dawn.

Our altar was of carved and gilded walnut, rather like a long mantelpiece, over which was set a glass fronted series of alcoves. The centre alcove contained a large image of Lord Buddha, and on either side of this were smaller alcoves containing images of divinities.

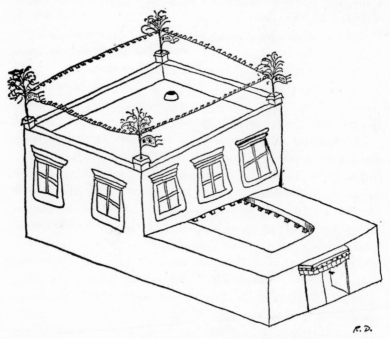

My house in Bhakar

This first daily task did not take Mother long and soon she was busy in the kitchen preparing the large cooked breakfast of stewed meat and potatoes seasoned with pickled turnip or cabbage, or perhaps plenty of eggs fried with onions; and always a lavish supply of steaming hot Tibetan tea, made with creamy tzomo or dri milk with a large nut of rich fresh butter beaten into it, the whole delicious mixture sharpened with a pinch or two of salt.

At second cock cry, my father and the men ate their breakfast quickly before hurrying out to the fields as the Dawn Star faded into the pale light of the approaching day. As well as crops, we had a lot of sheep, horses, goats and cattle to attend to. Like most Tibetan families our income was entirely derived from the infinite variety and profusion of the produce of our land; almost everything had to be home grown and processed. There was no time to be bored or idle; cattle and crops, like the tide, wait for no man!

When Father had left the house, at the first hint of sunrise Mother and my aunt gathered sprays of rhododendron leaves from the tall bushes that grew in abundance and carried them to the crest of a hill where every morning they lit a fire and prayed as the leaves smouldered into a fragrant incense which wafted their daily prayers to infinity.

On her way back to the house, my mother often paused to gather the luscious pastel-pink rhododendron blooms, still fresh with morning dew; or wild iris, rose or primula that grew in such colourful profusion in our valley. Mother loved beauty in her surroundings and our house was always gay with gleaming silver bowls full of spring and summer flowers or shining scarlet winter berries.

As soon as Mother returned from her daily prayers, the real work of the day began. It was time for my brother and me to get up and wash and dress while Mother prepared our breakfast. She had plenty to do with three big hot meals a day to prepare for the family, as well as a hot packed lunch for my father and the men when they were working a distant part of the farm. Then my young brother and I carried the food to them and enjoyed a picnic in the field with Father. One day, I remember, the lunch included deliciously golden, piping-hot chips. As my brother and I wandered along through the folds of the mountains towards my father we chatted happily, munching first one chip, then just another, then just one more until, when we finally arrived, we found to our alarm and great astonishment, when Father unpacked the lunch, there were only about half a dozen chips left! At first my father was rather displeased, but he was a gentle, understanding man with a great sense of humour, and in the middle of a scold he burst out laughing and told us we might as well finish them up as we had already eaten so many!

Tibetan food involves a good deal of preparation. Mother had no mincers or mixers, everything must be chopped very fine by hand; her stove had to be constantly fed with wood and dried dung, which burns fiercely and quickly. There was no popping out to the shops—the nearest shopping centre was Lhasa, almost three days ride away—so almost everything had to be home-grown and home-made. There was no need for a refrigerator, even had one been available. My home was 16,000 feet above sea level, the mountain air was clear and pure, there were no flies, and even in the summer when the days were warm the nights were very cold. Our storerooms were built of thick stone which kept them as cool and dark as the coldest cellar. Potatoes and onions we dug up as they were needed (this was often my job). Root vegetables, such as turnips, carrots, parsnips and swedes we stored in a specially dug ditch filled with loose soil. Meat hung by the carcase in the stores. One of my favourite snacks in winter, when the air was alive with frost, was frozen raw liver; left out overnight it was as crisp and crunchy as a water ice by morning and very delicious.

Most Tibetan food, including meat, is chopped very fine before it is cooked, and there is usually a variety of dishes at each meal: several kinds of chopped vegetables, homemade pickles, curds and in summer plenty of salad. Mother spent a good deal of her time every day preparing and cooking such meals for breakfast, lunch and supper.

There was a lot of cleaning and polishing to be done too. Everything in the house shone like a new pin, even our floors were as reflective as an unruffled lake. Our copper cooking pots were burnished after every meal, and silver lids and linings of our bowls sparkled like sunlit ice. We always used bowls of various sizes for our food, each one handmade and a work of art. Every Tibetan has his own tea bowl, which he takes everywhere with him. To be parted from one's tea bowl is the ultimate poverty and a sorrow to be avoided at all costs.

Bowl making, like pottery, is a craft handed down from

father to son; and the bowl maker was one of the itinerant traders who called occasionally and spent the day in our village.

I always enjoyed these visits. As well as their goods they brought news and gossip; some of them were fine story tellers too. My friend and I would watch enraptured as the bowl maker unloaded his selection of fine wood from his sturdy donkeys and settled down to fashion a beautiful piece of walnut or cherry into a perfect bowl, made to someone's specifications —perhaps a copy of an old favourite now worn out. In his expert hands the wood was soon as smooth and gleaming as satin; he had made my tea bowl from a beautiful piece of walnut and had lined it with silver before fashioning an exquisite silver design round the rim and fitting the silver lid to it exactly.

Pottery and tea we also obtained from visiting traders. The potters carried a selection of 'ready-made' pottery—the most beautifully designed and painted china came from Amdo, a far eastern province. But they too, like the bowl makers, could fashion any design from a description, so that a favourite teapot or flower vase could be reproduced many times. But to my mind, the most exciting callers were the Hørpas, the salt traders from Høre, a district in Kham. They were strong tough hardy men, with long black hair plaited closely round their heads, their gaze direct and their bearing proud as befitted men whose trade brought them many months of harsh travel over soaring passes across snow-choked mountains, battling blizzards and gales to bring salt to all parts of Tibet from the salt desert of the Chang-tang (the Great Plain), a bitterly cold, barren plateau in north-east Tibet. Their lives were full of hazards and adventures, and great was our excitement if one of them could be persuaded to tell us a story.

Whilst Mother was kept busy seeing to the meals for the family, my aunt was also fully occupied preparing the cloth for our clothes. Our sheep supplied the wool which she spun into yarn, easing and rubbing the fluffy loose wool with her fingers into a continuous thread which flowed gently through her left hand onto a constantly spinning wooden bobbin dangling loosely in front of her. When she had spun a good supply of yarn she sat at her loom for many an hour weaving it into thick, beautifully soft woollen cloth which my grandfather, old though he was, sewed expertly into chubas, shirts and trousers, all of which he lined with lambskins against the mountain cold. He dyed the cloth for our chubas from homemade vegetable dyes. Only the very poor wore white undyed chubas because dyeing was a complicated and expensive process. When grandfather had prepared the dye he often added some wild rhubarb to boil up with the cloth he was dyeing—the rhubarb helped to set the dye and make the material waterproof. It was sometimes my job to roam through the hills to gather the rhubarb. I enjoyed this and ate a good deal of what I collected as I walked along. The tartness made my mouth water and I recalled the story of the princes and the shepherd, all of whom desired to marry a beautiful princess. Her father, the king, decreed that her hand would be given in marriage to the suitor who could produce a meal that would make everyone's mouth water. Each prince in turn spent great sums of money on the most succulent foods to prepare the most delicious meals they could think of; each in turn sat before the king and an audience of courtiers to eat the meal that would make the onlookers' mouths water but none were successful. Then the King allowed the shepherd to have his chance. The onlookers smiled at the absurdity of a poor shepherd being able to afford a meal to make their mouths water. The shepherd smiled too and sat down before them to munch a large stick of wild rhubarb. Almost at once just the thought of the sharp sour taste made every watcher's mouth water. Even the King, swallowing hard, had to admit that the shepherd had produced the most mouth-watering meal of all and graciously gave his blessing to the marriage of the princess to the happy shepherd.

My days at home passed merrily and quickly. I was too young to be much help on the farm, and my brother and I had thousands of acres of fields and mountains to roam. A small boy's paradise of woods and streams to explore, trees and rocks and mountains to climb; every season brought its own delight.

In winter there was snow and ice for skating; in late spring and summer, camp in the higher mountains with the cattle; summer picnics and autumn harvesting when the winds grew stronger and more insistent, ideal for flying kites.

Most of the year round my friends and I played Boeli, a game like marbles only played with coins. Grown-ups did not altogether approve of this game, because it involved striking one coin with another and the coins were engraved with the Lion of Tibet; they felt it was somehow disrespectful, but all the same they did not protest very strongly and no disrespect was intended by the players.

In summer, when we tired of playing games, we wandered off to the stream that bustled gently along the side of the valley, the water sparkling like crystal in the brilliant sunshine. We would throw off our clothes and jump into the deliciously shocking icy water, catching our breath with the cold of it. Jumping and chasing and ducking each other we splashed and sang and laughed uproariously until the chill drove us onto the bank to run in the warm sun to dry ourselves and dress again.

The sun began to deepen towards sunset as we set off up the gentle hill that separated the stream from our village. When we crested the rise and skittered down the homeward slope, our homes lay before us like four white stones dropped casually onto a green and golden carpet. The sun sank quickly behind our backs, tipping the snow-crowned mountain peaks in scarlet and gold etched with purple, lengthening our shadows in front of us until we looked like slim giants in seven-league boots striding across our beautiful world.

So the days passed quickly, and if there were no games to play there was always mischief to get into!

Once I remember going into our haystore and finding some eggs laid by our wandering hens. I put all the eggs into my chuba pouch and came out of the store quickly. The Tibetan chuba, worn by everyone, is a very accommodating garment. It is an enveloping coat, drawn up to knee length and pouched over a belt; many things can be conveniently stashed away in this pouch round the waist. It was in my pouch that I put the eggs:

but I could not think how or where to eat them! First of course, they should be cooked; then I have to find myself a good place where I can hide myself and eat them. I was particularly fond of eggs and reflected that if I gave them to my mother she would only let me have one of these, whereas, if I kept them, I could eat all five—or so I thought at 6 years old! I wandered along looking for somewhere to hide and wondering how to cook them.

I was walking towards the mountains behind our house, thinking away, when suddenly there was a great fluster in the sky high above me. I looked up to see a huge lammergeier with a lamb in its talons being swooped on by a hungry rival. No matter how it tried to change its course to avoid the power-diving attacker the weight of its prey held it back. At first it clung strongly to the lamb as it tried to fend off the aggressor, but at last it was forced to return the attack; then the lamb slipped and dangled from one talon. Finally after a particularly ferocious attack, the eagle lost its grip altogether and the lamb tumbled like a limp white cloth through the sky to disappear into the thickly wooded slopes of the mountainside. The huge birds whirled in battle a moment longer, then the aggressor, seeing no lamb, lost interest and soared away into the distance. The defender spiralled a moment to catch its breath then flew on towards the rocky blue peaks that speared up through the mountain tree line.

In my interest in this sky-high battle I had forgotten all about the eggs tucked into my chuba pouch and I set off for home. The sun was fingering the mountains with rose-tipped rays and I knew it must be getting late.

Even when my mother came to put me to bed, I still did not remember the eggs! I loosened my chuba belt—and all the eggs fell on the floor and were broken!

My mother was angry and scolded me very much, but she was not angry enough to go and tell my father.

She asked me where I had got the eggs. I told her my friend's mother had given them to me. Of course I did not succeed in this answer because my friend's mother did not have any chickens! Then I could not think of anything else to say but the truth. I admitted I had taken them from our haystore. Mother was so pleased with me for telling her the truth that she told me I could have an egg next morning as a reward!

True to her word, for breakfast she gave me fried egg, butter, powdered cheese and pa (tsampa balls). Tsampa is a staple Tibetan food, it is finely powdered barley that can be mixed with any liquid, most frequently tea, to make a delicious and substantial food.

After breakfast, ever eager for eggs, I asked my mother if she would let me have another one if I went and found some more! She said I might certainly go and collect the eggs but if I ate too many I would never grow. She added (for good measure!) that if I remained small the owls would come and take my eyeballs. As I was very small for my age I took this warning quite seriously for a long time. There were many owls in the mountains round my home, especially on the very high mountain behind the house. I often lay awake at night listening to their "towhit-ooo", with my eyes screwed tightly shut for protection!

The day fades slowly in my country and the sky is light long after the sun has fallen below the mountains. It was nearly always late in the evening when Father returned from the fields; sometimes it was already starlight, but whatever the time, Mother always had the meal quite ready. As soon as Father was washed and ready, we all sat in a circle on thick rugs spread on the floor and Mother put the steaming pot of food in the centre, surrounded by many smaller bowls containing the 'side dishes' of vegetables and pickles. We all had our own eating bowls made for us by travelling craftsmen. Mine was made of gleaming Kongpo walnut lined with silver and with a scroll design in silver round the lip and base.

After supper I loved to sit on my father's lap, even when I was 6 years old. Sometimes in winter he would put his freezing hands on my face or down my chest and I can still remember how their coldness would nip like ice. Mother used to tell me not to sit on his lap, because he was always so tired after his long day's work, but I could never resist to do so.

Then Mother just smiled with gentle understanding as she moved about the room making sure the dishes were all polished and cleared away neatly.

When everything was tidy, Mother placed the firepan in the centre of our circle so that the glowing embers warmed us all. Then everyone found something to do. My aunt would spin or weave. As well as the cloth for our clothing she wove our thick blankets and the felt for our saddle cloths and boots, but these she wove from yak hair which is coarse and tough. Father and Uncle spun the yak hair into yarn; this is always men's work, the hair is far too harsh for women to spin, it would rub their fingers raw. Grandfather would put the finishing touches to some shirt or chuba he was making and Mother was very gifted with knitting and embroidery. Grandmother was very old and almost blind, she spent her time praying contentedly and smiling at our chatter, sometimes falling asleep in the warmth of the fire.

I always asked to be given something to do, but no one thought I was old enough. I was sure I could manage something, but no, I was never allowed. As everyone sat round the fire working in the lamp light we talked and told stories and sang for a while then said our prayers and soon it was time for bed.

Before we went upstairs the servants went down to unleash the dogs. As in all Tibetan houses, our living quarters were on the first and second floors; the ground floor was taken up with stores and stables. Our guard dogs ran loose during the night. They were as big as bears and very fierce; they had to be tied up during the day for safety.

Whenever a scorpion was found, which was quite often, it was always mixed with the dogs' meal of tsampa because it was believed that scorpions made all dogs very fierce and very brave! Our dogs ate a lot of scorpions. I can't say whether it really made any difference to them but they were certainly very fierce indeed!

Sometimes as a great treat, my mother arranged a cartoon film show for us after supper. We all took part in this. Mother cut out paper outlines of the heads of the characters in a play she would invent. Then we each stuck one of these paper silhouettes upright on the back of our hand, with our fingers held down towards our wrist, our thumb and little finger sticking out each side as arms. Perhaps one of us would wrap a piece of cloth round our wrist for a dress shadow to make a girl and two others would hold small pieces of wood to make sword shadows for a fight. We sat in front of the lamp and cast the shadows of our hand characters onto the wall. My mother was very clever at doing all the different voices and the singing for the various characters and our shadow actors were quite realistic!

I was always very reluctant to finish our cartoons when it was time for bed. I would beg my mother to invent 'just one more' and was usually successful; Mother was very kind and gentle and could rarely refuse me anything!

3

FOOTPRINTS IN THE FROST

In the spring following my fifth birthday, my father allowed me to go with our herds to the mountains for grazing. I was very pleased. It meant I could spend the whole summer high up in the mountains I loved so much. My father's brother, his wife and two shepherds packed up everything and loaded it onto yaks to take for our summer camp. Much of the way would be very steep and rough so the horses and mules were left behind, nor did we take the bullocks and cows because of their ineptitude at climbing. We also left some tzo to finish the ploughing.

The spring days sparkled with crisp sunlight and the green mountains glittered with early morning frosts. With the help of the dogs we drove the herds of yak, dri, tzomo, sheep and goats high up into the lush pastures of the bare mountains. The bare mountains of Tibet are covered with rich, tall, succulent grass and are so called to distinguish them from the many forested and rocky mountains. Some of the forest mountains are also covered in bushes with rush-like leaves from which we make baskets and with huge rhododendron and juniper trees, the leaves of which we burn as incense.

As the herds grazed on up the slopes in the early morning their footprints made patterns and funny drawings in the thick white frost cloaking the mountain. Following the herds I was completely engrossed in these frosted grass pictures until the heat of the rising sun dissolved them.

The site of our summer camp stood on a wide bank beside

a small blue lake about 20,000 feet up the mountain. As soon as we arrived our roomy yak-skin tent was put up and the work of the camp began.

My first job was picking mushrooms. There were a great many edible varieties, but I could only recognize two! One rather pretty yellow one we call sesha (golden mushroom) and the other a pure white one—but there were plenty of these and they tasted delicious fried or stewed for breakfast. There were also ptarmigan about and sometimes I found their eggs, which were also delicious.

Twice a day the dri and tzomo were tethered to a picket line for milking. They knew their particular halters and always made their way to their own place. Both animals give a large quantity of milk, but tzomo milk is particularly rich and creamy. We made curds, buttermilk, four different kinds of cheese and a great deal of butter which we packed tightly into dried Yak skins to store; butter packed like this will keep fresh for a very long time in the cool Tibetan air.

My aunt made all the butter in a large wooden cylinder which she half filled with milk, then, taking a flat wooden plunger with a perforated disc on the end, she plunged it many times up and down through the milk in the cylinder, singing special butter making songs to help her to keep the rhythm. I never tired of watching the butter begin to cream through the holes in the disc. When it was ready the contents of the cylinder was poured altogether into a big bowl, the butter was skimmed off and the remaining liquid made into cheese and buttermilk.

Every day my uncle and the shepherds went on foot to look after the herds. It was important to keep them as close together as possible. Everyone had to be very alert as at such altitudes unheralded low cloud could descend instantly and envelope everything in a damp impenetrable mist within seconds. Unwary cattle could be lost completely—falling down a hidden ravine, wandering over a mist-shrouded cliff—or be devoured by hungry, ever-present wolves always on the watch for straying cattle.

Sometimes my uncle took me with him and it was surprising

how far from camp the grazing herds would lead us before it was time to turn back. They were never allowed to roam the mountains unattended; wolves, leopards, bears and eagles would soon have a feast! At the end of a day with the herds I was usually very tired and as we made our way back to camp towards sunset my uncle often had to carry me.

On our return, the sheep and goats were herded into big pens made from the rushes of mountain bush and very strong. The yaks were separated from the dri and tzomo when they were all tethered to the picket lines and everyone set about the milking before darkness came.

By nightfall we were all very tired indeed, especially during the early summer when all the sheep had to be sheared. This was done either with scissors about the size of dressmaker's shears or with a kind of carving knife, according to taste. The fleece came off in one piece like a blanket. (In fact I always slept between two sheepskins in Tibet, the country is so high that once the sun goes down the nights are very cold even in summer.) The yaks and goats too must be groomed and their hair baled. So we were all very busy from Tho-rang-karchen until well after dusk—even later when the moon was full and bathed the camp with a marble white light as cool and silver as the day had been hot and golden. At full moon the night was as light as day, but when it waned, and if we were not too tired, we sometimes lit a piece of cloth surrounded by fat to nourish the flame, as a lamp. But more often the camp fire was enough to keep everyone warm and bright for as long as we were able to keep awake after our supper.

This summer passed very happily, and all too quickly it was time to gather the herds, the sheepskins, the bales, the butter, cheese and other fruits of our labours and return to the farm in time for the autumn harvesting.

This was a very busy time when everyone helped his neighbour to gather in the sheaves of corn, barley, wheat and rye. After all the sheaves had been stooked, they were loaded onto oxen to be taken to the threshing field. Our threshing field was directly behind our house—everyone tried to have their threshing field as near their house as possible, so that steaming hot meals could be brought out to the field. Some of our fields were a day's ride away. When my father and the men were working at this far end of the farm they took food and a tent with them and stayed for a day or two, eventually returning with the harvested grain quite late at night. The sheaves were stacked in huge blocks in the threshing field, and every member of the family took a hand in flailing the grain so that the chaff was carried away by the wind.

My first rides were taken at harvest time, on the back of an ox. I perched in the middle of a load of sheaves, very high up because even without their loads oxen are very tall, but there was no danger of falling off surrounded by the sheaves. By the time I was 5 I was allowed to ride the oxen without the protection of the sheaves.

I became very fond of riding and one day decided to ride one of our goats. It was a huge male goat, very handsome and dignified and usually very sweet tempered.

I saw him grazing quietly near the top of a deep ditch that in summer contained a brook that rushed down from the melting mountain snows with such rapid force that over the years it had carved quite a gorge; but now, in autumn, the waters of this torrent were already locked in ice in the snow mountains and there was nothing but a bed of dry sharp stones between the steep banks.

The morning air was singing with birds and sunshine. I had become bored with the threshing and wandered off in search of something more exciting to do. A ride on the goat was just what I was looking for. As I walked up to him, he did not seem to take much notice of me. I climbed onto his back, but I was no sooner aboard than he threw up his head in realization of what I had done. He didn't like it at all and started to run along the top of the bank. He ran so fast and so violently that he threw me head first into the dried-up gorge. One of the shepherds came and pulled me out but when he saw I had knocked a big hole in the back of my head and was bleeding profusely he ran away.

My head hurt very much, I could think of nothing to do but sit on the ground and cry. At last my father came along and found me. He lifted me on to his shoulder and carried me home, scolding the shepherd for letting me ride the goat. But it was not the shepherd's fault, I don't think he noticed me until I fell.

When we got to the house Mother made a flour ball and thrust it into the cut, which was very deep and large, to stop the bleeding. Then she tied it up with a chuba belt and Father took me to the nunnery on the side of a mountain about 2 miles away. In fact, the nunnery was actually inside the mountain; the rooms are deep natural caves, only the fourth or outside wall was man-made, of stone.

When we arrived one of the nuns first of all washed the cut with very cold water. This gave me a great deal of pain. Next she powdered about five jasangs. These are special pills made from clean soil and mixed into a paste before being blessed by a lama. Jasang is used a great deal in Tibet as a cure for many ills. The nun added water to the jasang, making it a yellowish cream; this she spread on my cut then tied it round again with the chuba belt. She gave my father about fifty jasangs and told him to wash the cut every morning then apply fresh jasang cream.

My head gave me terrible pain during the night, I cried bitterly and my father and mother became increasingly worried but did not know what to do. I could not sleep at all, the pain was so great I thought my head was going to explode. In the morning when my father washed the cut it felt as though he was hammering my head with an iron bar.

The cut grew worse and bigger until at last Father decided to call the village oracle man. In Tibet it is believed that there are a number of holy ghosts or spirits who influence the circumstances of the people for good or evil. It is believed that if someone in the family offends the holy ghost, the result will be some sickness or misfortune befalling the offending family as a reprimand. In this belief, the stricken family send for the oracle man, to find out, through him, the cause of their suffering and what reparations the holy ghost wishes them to make. So it was that as my head became worse, my father decided to find out who it was (in the opinion of the holy ghost) that had misbehaved, and he called the oracle man to tell him how the family could put the matter right. When the oracle arrived he dressed himself in the holy robes and my father beat the drums and cymbals as the spirit of the holy ghost entered into the body of the oracle man. The oracle said that one of the women of the household had put an apron on the stove and so one of the family must suffer, the retribution had apparently fallen upon me. My father apologized to the holy spirit, through the medium of the oracle man, and asked for forgiveness. The oracle replied that all would be well if my father lit 100 butter lamps as an offering. Then the holy ghost went away and the oracle man got his own spirit back.

Making 100 butter lamps was not a big problem for my father. We had a great deal of butter from our cattle and the family immediately offered the butter lamps at the nunnery, but my cut was not cured. The nuns told my father that he must continue to wash my cut in ice-cold water and dress it with jasang cream. At last, after two months, it was cured. I don't know whether the butter lamps or the jasang cured it; at any rate I was a strong healthy 5-year-old and perhaps nature just took its course. But by the time I started running about again, the threshing was finished and there were no yaks or oxen to ride down to the field.

It was the beginning of winter. The first snows had fallen and ice was everywhere. Not far from our house, near the crest of a foothill, there was a spring which never froze. The water flowed constantly down the hillside, spreading itself into a wide shallow sheet across the pasture below. In winter this thin film of water froze completely, the ice was so strong that it looked yellow and made an ideal natural skating and toboggan rink.

Tobogganing was one of my favourite sports. Every day I called for my friend and we set off for the hill. The sun shone brilliantly, the sky was sapphire and the air tight and crisp as we hurried along to find ourselves 'toboggans'. For these, we looked for large flat stones or sometimes hacked off a large piece of ice. We took our 'sleds' to the top of the hill, lay flat on our stomachs on top of them, gave ourselves a push and were off to the bottom and across the sheet ice of the pasture at a speed that really took our breath. Then up to the top of the hill again for another tremendous slide. I did this again and again until at last I was satisfied that my clothes were wet enough! I tried to get as wet through as possible in the hope that I would then get some new clothes to put on. Sometimes I was successful in this and as soon as I got something new I ran out to show the other children. One of them was sure to say that he must get something new to put on too, so we would again go toboggan-ing and get nice and wet.

The river, running fast and deep, was slower to freeze than the film of water across the pasture, but as soon as the ice began to form, off we would go and spend many hours cutting out very thin sheets of ice which we used to build glass houses, temples and even monasteries on the bank of the river. This game made us even wetter and dirtier than tobogganing and I would try to go to my father without my mother seeing me; but I never succeeded in doing this without her knowledge. She would send me to bed and there I had to stay until she had dried my clothes. When at last they were dry she would help me to dress and then tell me I must stay indoors; but I soon managed to slip out again. As I had no wish to be sent to bed twice in the same day, I played a drier cleaner game or two in the thresh-ing field, building bamboo huts or playing 'Guest and Host' with my friend. This time when I returned home in compara-tively clean clothes my mother would be so pleased, and perhaps surprised, that she gave me a bowl of hot, delicious dri milk as a reward for keeping my clothes dry.

As soon as the harvesting was finished, the grain was sewn into the sacks we had made from goats hair. Now we were ready to turn the mustard into oil for our lamps, the wheat into flour and the barley into tsampa.

Making tsampa requires considerable time and patience,

especially in the huge quantities that we made—sufficient for ourselves, my uncle's household in Lhasa, gifts for the nearby monastery and for a proportion of our taxes.

We built big outdoor stoves, kept sizzling hot with wood and dried dung, with as many vents as possible so that we could heat several pans of barley at one time and speed up the process. These pans were large and shallow, like copper frying pans, with miniature shafts into which a wooden handlebar could be inserted when the cooks wanted to lift them.

Once the stoves were hissing with heat, the bottom of the pans were covered with fine blue sand and as soon as this was really hot, small quantities of barley grain were poured into each pan. This was the exciting moment for me! The barley swelled and danced in the hot sand until at last it popped—like popcorn —and was done. As the pan was lifted off the vent another took its place, the cooked barley and sand from the lifted pan were poured through a very fine sieve held so that only the sand fell into the new pan and was reheated before more barley was added to be popped.

The sand was so fine it was impossible to hold it in your hand, it was the kind of 'running' sand I have seen used in Western egg-timers. We collected it from the river bank and it was a very pretty blue in colour.

As the barley was popped it was gathered into sacks and carried off by ox and yak to our grinding mill. This was built by a fast-flowing river which supplied the power for turning the grinding wheel, the speed could be controlled by a wooden sluice placed across the water like a lock gate. The popped barley was fed to the grinder through a chute, then the grain, completely powdered, filtered into waiting leather containers. The powdered tsampa was too fine to stow into sacks, it would have seeped out.

When all the barley had been ground into tsampa, the wheat was milled into flour.

Then the mustard and linseed was taken to another building, our 'vegetable oil refinery'! Here the seed was crushed and put into sacks to be steamed, then placed on racks over trays with a guttering type outlet which collected the oil pressed out of the steamed sacks by weights. The oil ran down the 'stone' gutters and dripped into storage pots, some to be used for lamps and some for cooking.

So, before the first snows of winter froze our land to stone, our harvest was truly completed and the storerooms safely filled with all our needs throughout the coming year.

4

THE GOLDEN ROOFS OF LHASA

Now I was 6 years old and my mother, who came from Lhasa, was keen for me to start school. There was no school or private tutor in the village: my mother did the reading and writing for everyone but had no time to give me regular lessons. So just after my sixth Losar—New Year birthday—it was decided I should go to my uncle, a government monk official at that time living in Lhasa, and I could go to school there.

I did not like this idea at all. Lhasa was two days and a night's journey by horseback from Bhakar, and I knew that once I went there I would be away from my home and my parents for a very long time. However, I had to go.

A day or two before I was to leave, my friends and I went on a tokchang. This is a picnic and tokchang means literally 'friend's chang' (Tibetan beer). But of course we were too young for beer, so my mother gave us meat, tsampa, butter, walnuts, fruit and tea.

We set off for the mountains, with a servant to do the cooking and see that we did not get into any mischief. In winter the grass of the bare mountains is dry and yellow; we had to be very careful lighting the campfire. Once some shepherds, lighting the fire for their tokchang, set the whole mountain alight and it blazed for several days. To guard against such a thing happening again, we gathered big blocks of ice, which we placed in a circle round the fire, so that the wind could not carry the flames to the dry grass.

We played games and ate an enormous meal, afterwards

talking very seriously about not very serious things, before going home tired but happy.

For a few hours, I had forgotten my sadness at the approaching parting from my parents.

All too soon the day of departure dawned and my father and I set off for Lhasa. I was still not allowed to ride alone, so I sat in front of Father, who also led another horse loaded with my clothes and possessions and two days' food supply.

In spite of my sadness at leaving my home I was at the same time quite excited to see Lhasa for the first time.

As we reached the edge of the plain that surrounds the city, the first thing I saw on the horizon were the golden rooftops of the Pota-la, the Palace of the Dalai Lama, shimmering in the dwindling sunlight. At first sight of the distant Pota-la, my father paused in our journey and prayed for me before we rode on across the plain into Lhasa.

It was getting late and very dark as we rode through the town. The moon had now set and I could see very little. We rode on for two or three miles until we came to Kundeling, where my uncle lived and which was now to be my home. Kundeling was a small village in the centre of a park, but in the darkness all I could really notice was that my uncle's house was the tallest. It was very late and I was tired after the long journey, so as soon as I had greeted my uncle, whom I was meeting for the first time, I went straight to bed.

In the morning when I went into one of the living rooms for my first breakfast I was quite struck by the size and beauty of the room. Our house in Bhakar was large and very nice but it certainly could not rival this. One whole wall of the room was a window with beautifully coloured designs painted on it. The decorated ceiling was supported by scarlet pillars which also had formal designs at the top of each of them. All the furniture too was carved and painted and it shone like glass— it was always polished twice a day every day—the entire room glistened in a flood of sunshine. Every room in the house had an altar and this one was no exception. All the altars had silver water bowls and golden butter lamps. The water bowls must be filled every morning and emptied every afternoon and then all the bowls must be polished. There were very many rooms and so of course many altars, so there were literally hundreds of bowls to be polished every day. The job of emptying and polishing the bowls was often given to me and it took me a long time to polish them all to the required perfection! After breakfast on my first morning, my uncle took Father and me to Jokhang, the main temple in Lhasa, often called the cathedral. We took with us some butter to add to the butter lamps and some money which by tradition we must leave in front of the image of Buddha as an offering. After my father and uncle had prayed for me, we went on up to the Pota-la to see the many temples it contains. Here for the first time I met another uncle, my uncle Nawang-la, who was Abbot of the Pota-la. I was to see him often in the days ahead, when he entertained me with many stories, whilst my uncle was engaged on government business in another part of the Pota-la which housed the government offices. (Uncle Nawang-la is still in Tibet and I have wondered many times what has become of him.)

As we walked round the Pota-la this first day I was too young and bewildered by the contrasts with my quiet home in Bhakar to appreciate much of the beauty and grace of the many lovely things we saw. But I was to go to the Pota-la almost every day during the next few weeks before starting school because my uncle had his office in the Palace, so of course he had to attend daily, not only on business but because it was customary for all government officers to attend early prayers at the Pota-la and pay their respects to His Holiness. I enjoyed these visits because I became very fond of my uncle Nawang-la, who had an endless fund of stories to keep me amused while I waited for my other uncle.

After walking round all the temples on this first day for what seemed to me to be an endlessly tiring time, we at last rode back to Kundeling—and I had my first real look at my new home.

I think perhaps one of the first things a foreign visitor would notice about a Tibetan house would be the shine, especially of the floors and furniture. My uncle's house was no exception. All the floors seemed to be made of mirrors reflecting the colours and shining furniture. Whether the floor was wood, as in some rooms, or of cement as in others, I could see myself reflected in them quite clearly. The floors are polished with candlewax which the servants spread thinly over the surface, then they polish them by constantly sliding their feet, encased in big felt overshoes, over the floor. The servants responsible for the gleaming floors do nothing else but ensure they maintain their glasslike appearance. But it makes the floors very slippery!

The house was white and three storeys high, built round a courtyard. All the living rooms, like the breakfast room, had a beautifully painted picture window in place of a wall on the courtyard side and the rooms were nearly always flooded with sunshine.

My father stayed with me for a week and took me into Lhasa to buy some 'city' clothes to replace my country ones. As I walked through the town in my homespun 'tweeds', children in the streets could see I was a country boy, they tried to tease me and called out to me. I was glad my father was with me to prevent them from teasing me too vigorously. I was very small and Lhasa seemed to me very big and noisy after the quiet security of my home.

There were not at this time many Chinese soldiers to be seen; it was 1952 and they had not yet started the policy of force and subjugation which was to come. There was very little traffic but a great deal of noise from a Chinese loudspeaker relaying Chinese music, I suppose for the entertainment of the passersby, although I doubt if they were really entertained, because most Chinese music sounds very monotonous and tuneless and is not at all like Tibetan music.

Occasionally a trader went by crying his wares in a ringing cadence, then a picturesque Hørpa singing "Salt for sale" or a smiling country peasant loaded with fresh vegetables.

The shops themselves had no shop windows; they were ordinary houses. Early every morning the shopkeeper placed a huge table in front of his house and arranged his merchandise on it in great profusion. Fortunately there is not much rain in Lhasa, but all the same there were gaily coloured canopies over all the tables to protect the goods displayed.

All too soon the week ended and it was time for my father to return to the farm. I said good-bye to him as bravely as I could and watched him ride out of sight, then I turned back to the house feeling very forlorn.

Now my brother began to look after me. I did not know him at all. He was almost fifteen years older than I and had been born in Lhasa where he had lived all his life with my uncle in Kundeling, and this was the first time I had ever seen him.

For many weeks after my father returned to Bhakar I was very unhappy indeed. I was hopelessly homesick and lonely and I felt very lost in the formal atmosphere of my uncle's house. I missed the warm, gay relaxed atmosphere of my home, the games and walks in the mountains, but most of all I missed my mother. My 6-year-old world seemed suddenly to have become a big and lonely place. There was nothing to do in the house; but I stayed indoors as much as possible to escape from the children in Kundeling who teased me when I went outside because they considered me a 'village boy'—a real country bumpkin.

Although my father had told my brother to look after me, we had a very difficult time for the first few weeks. For one thing we could not understand each other. At that time I spoke only Drekung dialect and my brother spoke only Lhasa dialect —which is very different. This did not help us at all to overcome the fact that we were complete strangers to each other and also so far apart in age.

However the days dragged by and at the end of a fortnight my uncle decided to send me to the small private school in Kundeling, about five minutes walk from the house. Here too I was very unhappy to begin with, I continued to be very homesick and the other children were teasing and unfriendly.

It was the custom, when a new boy entered the school, for his family to give a small party for the students and my uncle gave this party for me. First we had rice, tea and droma (a sweet seed always served as a traditional good luck sign). The rice too is a luxury party dish; it is not grown in Tibet and all imported foods are costly. We also had shamde, a thick soup made from rice, meat and sweet potato; then there were some small additional salads such as tomato, radish and onion: and of course the tea will go round continuously, all Tibetans are prodigious tea drinkers.

My party lasted all day and the students spent the time eating and chatting together. One or two of them came up and said something to me but we were strangers to each other and they were soon away again to rejoin their friends. At the end of the day, my uncle arranged traditional white scarves which I must give to everyone. First of all I must present one to the main teacher, then to his assistant and to the old monk and finally one to each of the students. As each one received a scarf they thanked me for the party. Some were more articulate than others and made quite a long speech but most of them just said thank you briefly.

I set off for my first day at school with anxious reluctance; I was not looking forward to it at all. When I arrived in the classroom, I was given an oblong wooden board and a cloth bag containing powdered chalk. This bag had a long string through the centre of it which I used for making lines on the board. To do this, I first moistened the board with ink (which was made from rye roasted black and then mixed with a little water) then I shook the chalk bag over it to make a powdery surface, finally I stretched the string horizontally and tightly across the board and flicked it sharply so that it made the lines. Now I was ready to write with my bamboo pen, sitting cross-legged on the floor like everyone else, with my board resting across my knees.

We had two teachers to teach us writing, a main teacher and his assistant. The first time I started to write it was the higher teacher who taught me, he always gave the first lesson to the newcomer.

He showed me how to hold the pen and guided my hand over the board. He did this three times. Then I must clean my board

The Tsangpo river, which flows 1,000 miles through Tibet before breaking through the Himalayas to become the Brahmaputra

A Tibetan village not far from Lhasa. The ruins of a Chinese fort can be seen

(above) The Pota-la, the Dalai Lama's monastery-palace at Lhasa

(below) A view across the Kyichu river towards Lhasa

with a drop of ink and prepare it all over again. This done, the teacher wrote some letters on the board, with a dry pen, for me to trace. When I finished writing over these letters I must show the teacher. This process was repeated until I was able to do it without his guide letters. When the main teacher was satisfied that I was writing nicely he gave me an enormous paper with the alphabet written on it, which I must copy out and then show to the assistant teacher.

Showing it to the assistant teacher could take a very long time! There was always a long queue of boys with their boards held in front of them, waiting to show the assistant, who some-times paused in his correction of our boards to sustain himself with a snack of dried meat or cake whilst we continued to stand in line, silent and motionless as instructed, as we watched him and waited.

On the first day, I did not do much more than learn how to prepare my board and try to accustom myself to my new sur-roundings.

After several days, my studies began in earnest. School started at six in the morning and ended at half past four in the after-noon six days a week. One of the servants called me at half past five, and after a breakfast of tea and tsampa I tucked a snack into my chuba for school break and set off.

School began with prayers. I did not know any prayers at this time, and, although I tucked myself away in a corner and kept quiet, the other boys noticed my ignorance and teased me about it.

The prayers lasted about half an hour and were followed by the chanting of mental arithmetic. These were tables and had a very nice tune to go with them. After this we memorized some basic grammar rules but without understanding them; they would be explained later when we moved on to grammar school.

To begin with I did not learn the grammar rules, but left the room immediately after the prayers to be taught the mental arithmetic chant by the assistant teacher.

There was also quite an old monk, who taught me four verses

D

of prayer each day. Although these lessons only lasted fifteen
minutes every morning, I had quite a lot to do to memorize the
daily verse and the arithmetic tables.

As in most primary schools writing the alphabet in large
letters was the first stage and these students had to write thirty
lines a day on their boards. As a newcomer I was expected to
write ten lines only, because some of my time was being taken
up with memorizing prayers and tables.

School studies, a very serious business

After completing each line of writing I must join the queue
of boys waiting to have their writing corrected by the assistant.
If any letter was not nicely made he wrote it on the next line
and perhaps a second corrected letter on the line below. I then
returned to my place and wrote these letters repeatedly along
the lines—but these lines of correction did not count in my ten
lines of writing to be done.

When my re-written letters were satisfactory I could then
go on to do the second line of writing; but first I must wash
and prepare my board again, taking great care not to erase the

number the teacher had written at the top of my board to mark how many lines of my daily quota I had already completed to his satisfaction. Sometimes I forgot and rubbed out this number by mistake when I cleaned my board; it was not too bad if I forgot and rubbed it out in the morning when it indicated I had completed one or two lines; but it was very tiresome when I forgot in the afternoon and had perhaps only one more line to complete, because then I had to do the whole day's quota over again and this took a great deal of time and patience. This was particularly discouraging as I progressed and my daily quota increased to thirty and finally fifty lines!

Lunch was provided at the school and there was usually a little time left for play before the hour was up but I still did not know the Lhasa dialect and could not understand what the boys said, which made them laugh and made me miserable. I had to teach myself the dialect but the honorific form was always used in Uncle's house and I learnt this quite quickly.

When school finished at half past four, I took my full number of writing lines on my board back for my uncle to see. He always checked them all very carefully to be sure I had done them nicely.

I had supper with my uncle and my brother and two other uncles who lived with us. One of them was quite old, the eldest of my mother's sixteen brothers; the other one was about 25 and was later taken to China and we never saw him again.

After supper every evening my uncle would hear my arithmetic verses. I had to repeat them many, many times. He was very strict and kept me beside him, repeating the verses over and over again very quickly for an hour, or sometimes two, until I thought he would never let me go. At last guests would arrive to play mahjong and I would be released to go to bed. Mahjong was a favourite pastime in Lhasa, but I was never allowed to watch or play, because my uncle was afraid I would be tempted to become a gambler. Gambling was very popular in Tibet.

One morning, soon after I started at school, I found a small empty tin in the street as I walked to school very early in the morning and from that day I enjoyed my walk to school very much kicking this tin ahead of me. It made a splendid noise and became a great friend to me. Sometimes it fell into a deep ditch beside the road, then I had to climb down and retrieve it, I did not want to lose it. When I arrived at school I hid my tin under the stairs where nobody would find it and when I got back to my uncle's house in the evening I hid it under our stairs. It was very dark there and I knew no one would find it.

I kept this tin until I went to Norbulingka to another school, three months later, and I can still recall the joy and sense of companionship it gave me.

5

AUTUMN KITES

A T the end of three months I left the school in Kundeling to go to a small private school in Norbulingka. There were ten of us at this school and we all boarded. My school day was still very long. We started with prayers at six in the morning; then we swept and tidied our rooms, five of us to each room, before starting our lessons which continued all day until we finished with prayers and bed at nine at night.

There were no kindergartens or play schools in Tibet, such as there are in the West; schooling was a very serious matter and even the smallest children must study very hard.

The Norbulingka or Jewel Park, was His Holiness the Dalai Lama's favourite park, and it was here that the new Summer Palace was being built under the supervision of my uncle. My school was in Chenseling, a smaller park within the Norbulingka.

By now I had learnt the Lhasa dialect quite well and was also becoming quite fluent with the honorific because we always spoke this in Uncle's house; but in spite of being better able to communicate with my fellow students and my brother, I was still very homesick. We had to study very hard. Our schooling was not divided up into terms as in the West—our longest holiday was the fortnight for Tibetan New Year (Losar)—but we had quite a lot of free days. There were many 'Bank Holidays' in Tibet: every 8th, 15th, 30th and every Sunday. There were also holy days and religious ceremonies and at all these times I returned to Kundeling, which was not very far away. On the frequent ceremony days my uncle took me to the Pota-la and the Jokhang to offer butter lamps and money at the many temples.

Sometimes our school challenged another to a Kite Tournament. This was a very serious business! We would write: "We challenge you to a kite duel on Friday 13th. We will be flying beard kites. Kindly let us know what kites you will be flying."

Flying kites was an immensely popular sport. Autumn was the kite season. In summer it was forbidden because superstition had it that flying kites in summer prevented rain in winter. Since there is very little rain in Tibet and practically none at all in Lhasa itself, this superstition was taken very seriously.

Everyone made their own kites, usually square in shape, using thin, strong paper. They were decorated with patterns which had become recognized kite designs. The beard kite was always black and white; the red-eyed kite had two red circles; the wheel kite had a big wheel drawn in the centre, and so on.

The object of the tournaments, or duels, was for each kite handler to destroy as many of his opponents kites in the air as possible. To do this not only involved great expertise in directing the flight of the kite but hours of painstaking preparation beforehand. The tension and suppleness of the bamboo blades used to stretch the paper of the kite must be just right—too tight and the paper will tear; too weak, the paper will not be taut enough—but most important was the preparation of the string.

First of all, some glass must be collected, usually empty bottles. These must be broken and pounded into a very fine powder. You must be careful not to cut your fingers and your eyes must be shielded from any flying splinters by wearing travelling goggles or strips of silk across your eyes. Once the glass was powdered finer than castor sugar it was well mixed with plenty of glue in a bowl.

Now you were ready to prepare the all-important part—the string you intended to attach to your kite for the competition. There were five or six big reels of strong cotton thread to be

treated with the glass and glue mixture so you settled down to
a long afternoon's work! A small wire was threaded through
the centre of each reel, then the thread could be drawn evenly
through the mixture so that it became evenly coated with the
powdered glass and then laid out carefully to dry before being
wound onto a big wooden spool which revolved on a rod thrust
through the centre; the kite could then be controlled by pressure

Kite tournament competitions are very keen

against the sides of the spool. Now the kite was ready for
action!

There were a number of stratagems that could be used to
bring down opposing kites. A 'knock on the head' involved
manœuvring your kite until it was high above the kite you
planned to dispose of; once in position (and it could take time as
well as skill to achieve the exact angle) you brought your kite
down in a steep fast dive onto your opponent's kite. If the dive
has been accurately judged, the paper of his kite will be ripped
and it will fall to the ground. In other words it will have been
'knocked on the head'. In the 'cut' the idea was to guide your

kite across the opponent's kite string so that the sharp, powdered glass of your own string cut through his; when this ploy succeeded you shouted loudly, 'I have cut it!' and joyfully chalked up your score.

The tricky part of 'flying' could sometimes be that you had no idea whose kites you were pulling out of the sky because the handlers were so scattered about. Of course you could tell during a tournament because you knew what type of kites your opponents had agreed to fly for the competition. But there were also private 'flying parties', or you could be flying your kite quietly alone when you spotted another kite flying quietly towards you. The impulse to try and cut this intruder loose was irresistible, if you were successful there was great exhilaration in watching the freed kite soar higher and higher into the distance, also some excitement in wondering whose kite it was you had so successfully challenged, for it could be almost anyone from a senior monk to a peasant, so universally popular was the sport—but the embarrassment belonged to the vanquished for losing his kite!

The biggest day of all for kite enthusiasts was 'National Kite Day'. Then all Lhasa was *en fete* to entertain the happy crowds of people, all dressed in their best clothes, enjoying a gay day out, excitedly supporting the various teams taking part in the competitions; thronging the sideshows and shooting galleries; trying their skill at throwing rings over small gifts; and in general all the fun of the fair. There were sweet tea sellers, cake stalls and small tent restaurants to supply refreshment and for many families it was a last picnic in one of the beautiful parks beside the Kyichu river or on the banks of one of the ornamental lakes, before the weather chilled with the icy winds of winter.

There was no school that day so I joined the other children on one of my rare 'days out' in Lhasa, thoroughly enjoying the excitement and sense of freedom I experienced as I wandered through the gay crowds, trying my luck at the sideshows and watching vanquished kites disappear into the sky.

The Tibetan Calendar is arranged according to the stars and the moon. When the moon is full it is always the 15th or the

30th of each month. This system makes each month consist of thirty days, so it can be seen that we sometimes have some days over, because the phases of the moon do not fit regularly into fifteen day cycles. To overcome this, we occasionally have double dates, perhaps two 10ths or two 24ths or what have you, and sometimes even a double month! This system also makes our New Year, Losar, a movable feast, although it usually falls towards the end of the Western February. Losar is not only Tibetan New Year but is also every Tibetans' birthday, so it can be imagined that it is a fortnight of tremendous activity. A little before Losar, on the 29th day of the twelfth month, we have Guthuk, which is a sort of New Year's Eve. To prepare for Guthuk chimneys are swept, houses are cleaned from top to bottom and Kapse (Tibetan cakes) are baked. All must be spotless and finished by the 29th; in the same tradition as the Scottish Hogmanay, there must be no speck of the old year's dust left when we herald in the New Year.

The word Guthuk means Nine Tuppa. On the 29th each person must eat nine bowls of tuppa to bring him good fortune during the coming year. Our tuppa (a thick soup) contains lucky symbols, like the Western Christmas pudding. These symbols are small balls of flour, each of which contains either a piece of charcoal, a little salt, string, white wool or a flour shape of a sun or moon. Like sixpences and charms in Christmas pudding, these flour balls are dropped into the big bowl of tuppa and a person may be served with several in his bowl or perhaps none, according to chance. The contents of each flour ball indicates a prediction for the coming year.

The one who gets the charcoal will be the 'black sheep' of the family, but for the coming year only! The one who gets the pepper will be the chatterbox! The salt predicts laziness and so on.

From the day following Guthuk we are all very busy making our preparations and decorations for the New Year.

I spent the New Year holiday at Kundeling, and although I felt rather homesick I found the celebrations exciting. It is the custom for children to go to bed very early on the New Year's

Eve whilst the adults arrange everything for the coming day. While the children are sleeping, new clothes from head to toe are placed secretly on their pillows.

On New Year's Eve, of course, I pretended to sleep, but with one eye open to see what clothes were being put on my pillow. To me it was a most exciting moment as I felt, rather than saw, my new clothes being put beside me. I lay in the dark for what seemed a terribly long time before someone came to give me permission to get up and put on my new clothes. But first I had to exchange our traditional New Year greetings, wishing good luck for the three blessings: long life, happiness, and peace. Only then could I at last jump out of my bed and put on my new clothes. It was still very early in the morning and very dark as I went to our sitting-room, feeling very smart, for traditional New Year breakfast. After exchanging greetings with my uncles and brother we sat down to our special Losar breakfast.

After this my uncle had to go to the Pota-la to attend the official government ceremony. He told me to accompany him. It was still dark and very early as we came down the stairs and out into the courtyard. My uncle's horse was saddled and waiting; beside it was a half-grown roan pony wearing a shining walnut-wood saddle beautifully decorated with intricate silver designs. Imagine my joy on being told that the pony and saddle were a Losar gift from my uncle for my seventh birthday. What was almost more exciting was that this lovely gift meant I would at last be allowed to ride by myself on my own pony instead of up in front of my uncle on his horse. I christened my pony Dolma and we rode off to the Pota-la. I thought I would burst with the joy and excitement of my new clothes, new saddle and new pony.

When we had exchanged New Year greetings with everyone at the Pota-la my uncle went off to the government officials' ceremony and I spent the long wait with my other uncle, the abbot, in his *tasha* (sitting-room) listening to the stories he was always so ready to tell me, and the time passed very pleasantly until it was time to join everybody and watch the special performance of historical dances traditionally performed by the lamas. These dances continued for almost the entire day, but we did not stay very long. My uncle wanted to get back to Kundeling to receive his guests, although strictly speaking New Year's Day itself is more for the family and close relatives to be together and for the religious ceremonies. In most households it is not until the second and third day of Losar that friends and acquaintances come to call.

On our return to the house I was very reluctant to part from my new pony, but I had to join my uncle and sit quietly whilst he entertained his guests. I felt very restless sitting there. I was eager to go out to play and show some of my new friends my beautiful pony but I did not know how to escape from the grown-ups and my uncle did not think to let me go.

This particular Losar I really felt very self-conscious and uncomfortable because I was half bald! Just before New Year, when I arrived from Norbulingka to start my Losar holidays, my hair was rather long and my brother decided to cut it. We had a pair of clippers in the house and I suppose my brother wanted to see how they worked. He started to cut my hair with them and it looked terrible! He did only one side of my head but the clippers shaved this half completely. When he saw how the clippers worked and that I now had hair on only one side of my head he jammed a hat on my head and hurried me to the barber. To speed the way we went on the bicycle. This was the first time I had ever been on a bicycle and as I sat on the crossbar in front of my brother I was very alarmed and giddy. Although I knew we must be moving down the road, it felt as though we were stationary and that the trees and electricity poles were dashing towards me at a frightening speed, it seemed as though the whole countryside was revolving. I was relieved and honestly surprised when we arrived at the barber's shop safely. Once inside and sitting on the chair in front of the mirror I saw my 'hair cut' for the first time and I was very upset at the spectacle I presented. One side of my head was as bald as an egg, the other side still a mass of thick black hair. I was quite despondent but the barber was filled with laughter

at the sight of me and it was some time before he could stop
the tears of amusement rolling down his fat good-natured face.
The only solution was to shave the other side of my head to
match the bald side and the result made me look like an egg. I
was very upset.

The return journey on the bicycle was much worse. Part of
the way led down a very steep zigzag hill, and as we sped and
twisted downwards my stomach dropped suddenly as if we were
flying, the trees rushing towards us seemed only to get out of
our way at the very last moment. I felt as though I was spinning round and round in a vast tree-lined cylinder and it made
me feel giddy and rather sick. I was immensely relieved when
we arrived at the house without accident.

My uncle was quite pleased with my shaved head because, as
a monk, his head was also shaved and I suppose he thought
that now he had company! I was not at all pleased; the barber
had used a cut-throat razor and shaved my head very close
indeed. As well as looking terrible, it was also very uncomfortable and it was a long time before my hair even started to grow
again. I was very miserable and wore a hat all the time as far
as I could. It really quite spoilt the holiday for me.

On the third day of Losar we set off for Medical College Hill.
This was the day when everyone climbed the mountain of
Chakpuri (Iron Hill) to place their prayer flags at the top.
Hundreds of people, from many miles around climbed the hill to
bring their flags. By the end of the day the mountain top was
brilliant with the multitude of brightly coloured new prayer
flags fluttering gaily in the brisk wind. This traditional climb
to the top of Chakpuri marked the end of most of the Losar
celebrations, and the rest of my two weeks holiday was spent
very quietly.

By this time I had made one or two friends and they liked to
come to my house to play hide and seek. My house was especially popular because we had plenty of room. There were
stables and storerooms and most particularly three big empty
rooms which were very dark; the darkness added a delicious
shuddery creepiness to both hiding and seeking.

We were not allowed to play Boeli at Losar, but as a change from hide and seek we sometimes played Apchuk, a sort of skittles played with dried and gaily-coloured animal bones.

There were many beautiful public gardens and parks in Lhasa. My uncle's house stood in the centre of Kundeling (ling is Tibetan for park) and during my holiday I spent many pleasant hours enjoying the vivid colours and scents of the flowers that grew in abundance. One of my favourite pastimes had always been to sit quietly and observe the many patterns and designs of nature. Lying on the grass in the shade of a willow tree I would watch a spider trap and bind her prey to stock her larder; follow the ants hurrying to and fro, sometimes moving house in an incredibly short time, each one carrying an egg as big as itself.

Tibetans do not fish, so the translucent waters of the rivers and lakes were full of fish. I could lie on a bank and watch them flow through the water as clearly as if they were in an aquarium. They were really quite tame and would rise at once for any food they were offered. Like the birds and most wild things in Tibet, they had no reason to fear man because they were not hunted. Tibetans never kill anything except in self-defence or self-preservation.

Very occasionally snow fell in Lhasa, usually just before or after Losar. Then my uncle might decide to give a snow party. I would eagerly volunteer to go into the park to collect the necessary snow for the 'invitation'. I took enough snow to make a hard-packed fair-sized snowball which was then care-fully packed into a nice parcel and given to a servant to take to the chosen friend. Great care had to be taken in selecting the servant for this, because much depended on his presentation of the parcel. He must offer the parcel as a gift and be as con-vincing as possible; no matter how firmly the intended recipient declined the 'present' it was the servant's duty to insist on his acceptance, for if he did not succeed in this and had to return the parcel unopened to my uncle, it meant that my uncle must give the party, if the servant could persuade the other man to accept the parcel then this man must be the host to my uncle.

This of course was the object of a 'snow party'. For this reason, when snow had fallen in Lhasa, everyone was very cautious about accepting 'gift parcels' from their friends! But whether the parcel was accepted or returned, rare snowfalls always resulted in a bout of parties!

Of course I was too young to attend these parties, but I enjoyed collecting the snow for the parcel, and when my uncle was involved in a snow party it meant I did not have to spend so much time reciting my lessons to him, so I enjoyed the parties too!

6

THE ROAD HOME

I HAD been in Kundeling just over a year when my mother
came to Lhasa for a week, bringing my younger brother with
her. He was to be settled in the Pota-la to study with my uncle,
the abbot, and become a monk. During Mother's visit they
stayed at Kundeling and I was given a week's holiday from
school to be with them. I was almost beside myself with joy
to see her again and my mother was, of course, very pleased to
see me; but my younger brother seemed more puzzled than
pleased by the sight of me and hid behind Mother. He was very
young and had probably almost forgotten me during the year
since I had left my home.

My mother brought me a thick country chuba and a string
of chugum. I was delighted. The chuba was beautiful and the
chugum delicious. Chugum is a very creamy cheese cut into
squares and threaded onto a string, like rosary beads. It dries
almost rock solid and keeps for a very long time. It is particularly popular with traders; they find it sustaining on their long
journeys and chew it like Western chewing gum.

Mother was very busy during her brief stay in Lhasa; it was
her home town and she had been away a long time. She had
many brothers and sisters and old friends to visit and took me
everywhere with her. She bought me small packets of sweets
which she gave me one by one telling me I must make them
last; but they were a great treat and making them last was too
difficult; crunching them up at once, I was immediately ready
for another.

Almost before I had fully realized that my mother was really in Lhasa with me it was the end of the week and time for her to go home again. On the day of her departure we left my younger brother at the Pota-la and then it was my turn to say good-bye to her. It was a sad parting and we both wept as she promised to come and see me sometimes.

I went back to Norbulingka on foot. It was a very desolate walk and I was not at all pleased to be back at school.

Not long after I got back to school, it was my turn to sweep and clean our room. In Tibet we used big yak-skin bags as dust-pans. The farmers stuffed their butter into whole yak skins for sale in the market. This skinful of butter was then cut in half and when all the butter was used the skins retained their shape and made large but rather hairy dustpans.

This day I emptied our dustpan upside down on the lavatory and left it there whilst I went back to finish cleaning the room. I forgot all about it.

Much later, just before we all went to bed, our teacher went to the lavatory. There was no light in there and in the darkness he was very frightened to see a big hairy shape apparently sitting on the lavatory—I think he thought it was a ghost. At any rate he came out again very quickly calling to one of his servants to bring an oil lamp. When the lamp was brought he saw at once that it was the upturned dustpan and was very, very angry. He sent one of the government sweepers into the park to pick four canes whilst he set out to discover the culprit and punish him. He quickly discovered that I was the guilty one because it was my turn to do the sweeping upstairs, but by this time I had run downstairs to try to escape notice. I did not know that one of the servants had gone to the teacher to ask him to excuse my forgetfulness. Although it was now very late and dark I decided that it was better to run away than stay and be punished. Breathlessly I slipped into the park and started to run towards the main gates. As I ran, I could hear the Dalai Lama's bodyguards on night watch. Suddenly one of them heard me and shouted, "Who are you?" "I am a Chen-

A crowded Lhasa street scene. In the distance, from left to right, Chakpuri (the Medical College), Tzuklakang (Lhasa Cathedral, including Jokhang Temple) and the Pota-la

The author's teacher in Norbulingka is on the extreme left of this group

Two High Lamas, respected scholars and teachers

saling student" I shouted back. He could not see me in the pitch dark and I carefully kept my distance as I explained, "I am going to get some dried manure for the fire!" He believed me and I ran on, but then I suddenly remembered that the gates of Norbulingka were locked at seven for the night and there was no passing through until morning. I hurried on trying to think of a good place to hide until the gates were unlocked at dawn. Suddenly I stumbled over something in the dark and discovered I had blundered into a mass of thick, long beams piled ready for use on the new palace being built for His Holiness. I found a space under the beams and crawled inside, but in spite of my warm clothes and lambskin-lined chuba I was bitterly cold. I could not sleep for shivering not only with cold but with the fear of discovery. It seemed even colder in my dark space in the beams than it was outside; the wind drove through the gaps between the beams like a thrusting sword and cut me to the bone. But at last the sky grew lighter as the night lifted and I crept from my hiding place, stiff and hungry, but still determined to run away.

There was no one about in the park at such an early hour and I reached the gates quite safely, only to find they were still closed. I found myself a comfortable place in a nearby shrubbery where I could wait for the gates to open without being seen. I waited quite a long time, but at last as the sun tipped over the mountains, the gates were opened and I slipped through unnoticed. The gates are guarded by two huge stone statues of the Lions of Tibet and I was just walking between them with all fears of discovery banished, when someone came up behind me and my heart leapt into my throat as he grabbed my hand. It was one of the Khebah (government sweepers), he had been waiting behind one of the lions expecting me to come by. He was a very nice, rather old man and as we walked back to Chensaling together he talked to me like a father, pointing out that running away was no solution, I must continue my studies, he told me, otherwise I would become nothing more than a sweeper as he was. Tearfully I told him about the dust-pan and the punishment awaiting me if I returned to school.

E

He was very kind but continued to hold me firmly by the hand as we walked relentlessly back. He advised me not to worry and promised to see the teacher to explain everything to him, assuring me that all would be well and punishment forgotten. I did not feel so sure but by this time we had arrived back at school and the old man sent me into the kitchen to have a cup of tea and wait whilst he went to speak to the teacher. I felt very anxious and it seemed a long time before I was at last told to go upstairs. As I entered the classroom it seemed as though everyone was holding their breath in anticipation of the storm about to break but the teacher said nothing more than "Where did you sleep last night?" and made no comment whatsoever when I told him of my night in the park. I have no idea what the old Khebah had said on my behalf, but he must have been a fine advocate and I was relieved to be allowed to sit down in the class without more ado.

About a week after this episode my big brother came from Kundeling to tell me that my younger brother had run away from the Pota-la and no one knew where he had gone. He was not yet 6 years old and everyone was naturally rather worried.

It occurred to me that my brother had probably run back home to Bhakar and that it would not be a bad idea if I went too. I had never overcome my homesickness and since my mother's visit to Lhasa I missed my home more than ever. I began to consider the possibilities of running away home very seriously and about a week after I first had the idea, the chance presented itself.

My teacher handed me his snuff pot and told me to go to Kundeling and bring him some of my uncle's special snuff, which was a favourite blend of his. Here was my chance and I set off very willingly, feeling excited but also a little nervous at the thought of what I was planning.

I did not go to Kundeling at all but ran straight to Lhasa and Chaksam, the iron bridge the Chinese had built across Kyichu river, which separated the town from the main north-east highway I must take at first. The entrance to the bridge was guarded by two Chinese soldiers with rifles, and as I saw them lounging outside their sentry boxes my heart sank. They will never let me pass, I thought and was just deciding to wait for a chance to slip through unnoticed when I saw a Pungoh (man who looks after donkeys) approaching the bridge with a group of saddled donkeys. I noticed that the Chinese let him pass on to the bridge unchallenged and this gave me an idea. I waited out of sight until the Pungoh had driven his donkeys almost to the centre of the bridge, then I started quickly after him.

As I stepped onto the bridge, one of the guards stood in front of me and lowered his rifle right into my stomach. I was very frightened but stood my ground and pointed urgently towards the Pungoh, pantomiming that he was my father and I must hurry after him. The Chinese lowered his rifle (perhaps he had only been joking) and allowed me to go through the barrier onto the bridge. I was very relieved and started running as though to catch up with the Pungoh. I ran very fast and soon after crossing the bridge I overtook the donkeys and left the Pungoh far behind.

The road was good, it was the main motor road from Lhasa to Eastern Tibet and I could follow it northwards for some way before it turned east at Medoh Kongka. The road ran flat and straight across the plain, the surface was smooth and running was easy. I could see Lhasa and the glinting rooftops of the Pota-la as I frequently looked back, fearful of pursuit. The plain was unobstructed and I felt very exposed in such an expanse. I never slackened my pace, the sun had not yet gone down and I wanted to travel as far as possible while the light was still clear. I continued to run until it was quite dark and when at last I decided to stop for the night there was not a house in sight and no shelter of any kind, not even a bush. It was useless to think of stopping unsheltered by the roadside; not only would it be bitterly cold but I would be found immediately, either by the Chinese who used the road a great deal or by possible pursuers from the school where my absence would surely have been marked by now. There was nothing for it but to run on in the increasing darkness and hope to find somewhere safe to rest.

I had not run much farther before I came to a narrow bridge over an irrigation ditch that crossed the road. The ditch was dry and when I jumped into it I found that the bridge was formed by a fair-sized cylinder which in summer would pipe the ditch water under the road but which now was quite dry because it was winter. I crawled inside it and felt quite snug but still rather afraid that I might be caught. Nevertheless, in spite of this fear, I was very tired and soon fell asleep.

I don't know how long I had been sleeping when I awoke with a tremendous start. It was pitch dark and I seemed to be completely engulfed in a tumultuous noise; the tunnel was shaking and clanging about me with the most fearful din. I clambered out quickly in a great fright, just in time to see the rear lights of a Chinese truck disappearing in the distance. I realized that the tumult in my tunnel must have been caused by the truck passing over the metal immediately above my head.

It was still too dark to see the road properly so I got back into the tunnel intending to sleep again, but my mind was too full of fear at the possibility of being caught; then the memory of the ghosts my brother used to tell me about at Kundeling made me even more fearful and I was thankful when at last it grew light enough for me to start on my way again. It was extremely cold so early in the morning but I set off at a good pace and running soon warmed me up. As on the previous day I had no food, but the road ran alongside the Kyichu and I stopped several times to drink the cool clear water. I ran on across the plain towards the mountains and at last the land began to rise steeply on either side of me as I reached the foot-hills. I began to feel more sheltered from discovery now that I could no longer be seen from any great distance. The road wound with the river along the foot of the hills and I hurried on until the long twilight began to deepen into darkness. I had passed through several villages earlier in the day—groups of three, sometimes four, houses set well back from the road. Apart from reluctance to go out of my way I had wanted to avoid inevitable explanations and the possibility of being summarily returned to school, which I feared would follow a call at any house *en route*. Now it was getting quite dark and I was tired and hungry but the bare grass mountains on either side of the road offered no shelter from the increasing cold and rising wind. I walked on feeling rather disconsolate, when to my delight, as I rounded a bend, I saw the warm glow of lamplit windows ahead of me. Here, I thought, I can find a stable or storeroom to sleep in. I quickened my pace in anticipation of a good sheltered sleep and warmth, it was really very cold now and the wind was thrusting past me with glacial blasts. I hurried along towards the lights, and as I drew nearer I could see that there were twenty or thirty houses. I felt a thrill of delight as I realized I had reached Medoh Kongka, which meant that I was a little over half-way home and had only about another 30 miles to go. With this happy thought I trotted into the village light-heartedly—and rather incautiously. Rounding the corner of a house in search of a hiding place I ran straight into a man returning late from work in his fields. He must have realized I was running away. In that sparsely populated area anyone unfamiliar was undoubtedly a stranger and any unknown small boy must be running away! Fortunately he was very kind and took me to his home, where I was immediately given a large bowl of steaming hot tuppa. I was ravenous and very ready for a second helping when it was offered! It was the first food I had eaten since leaving Chensaling two days before.

It was quite a big house, but there were seven children in the family and they had no spare room, so the man put me in their haystall to sleep. It was so hot there that I did not need any blankets. I covered myself with hay and fell asleep immediately.

Next morning, after several cups of butter tea and another big bowl of tuppa, I set off on my journey refreshed and fortified against the cold.

Now the going was not so easy. I had to leave the motor road which turned away to the east and cross the river to cut across country to the north. I did not know how to cross the river. At this time of year it was not very deep, the waters that fed it were still locked in the mountain snows, but it was still very wide, too deep to wade and too fast-flowing to swim. Here was a problem and I sat down on the bank to try to puzzle it out.

I had been sitting for some time searching unsuccessfully for a solution when a boy about 12 came along with some oxen. All of them had wooden saddles and as soon as the boy heard of my difficulty he at once suggested that I ride one of them. I didn't hesitate, I jumped quickly on to the nearest ox, who carried me safely and smoothly across. Once on the opposite bank, I thanked the boy for his help and went on my way.

Now I was safely across the river, I no longer feared pursuit, but the route was more difficult, and I was not too sure of the way. The first and last time I had made the journey was when my father had taken me to school in Lhasa and that seemed a long time ago. But I knew I must leave the river as it flowed away to my right and travel as best I could in a straight line almost due north. I followed a path which threaded its way through foothills interlocked like green fingers. As I rounded each incline another lay before me and another beyond that, sometimes outlined with bush or juniper and always un-familiar. Many times another path led into the distance to left or right and I hesitated and wondered if it led to our valley, but each time I decided I must keep straight on. It was getting dark and I was tired and disheartened when I rounded yet another foothill for what seemed like the hundredth time and there at last, in front of me, was our village.

Filled with excitement I started to run down the valley. As I ran I could see that the animals had all come down from the mountains for the night and everyone was busy tethering them for milking.

Then quite suddenly my excitement changed to alarm as I realized, for the very first time, that it had never occurred to me to wonder what my parents would say when they saw me and heard I had run away. This was indeed an appalling thought and I sat down a short distance from the house to try and devise an explanation—but with no success.

I had been sitting there, racking my brains for some reasonable excuse, for what seemed a long time, when at last my mother came out of the house and saw me. With a cry of delight she came running towards me. Lifting me up she hugged me tightly and we both cried with joy. We walked into the house together and there was my father. In spite of the fact that they had both been praising me to my younger brother for not joining him in running away, my father was as pleased to see me as my mother was and I was filled with happiness to be home again.

My younger brother had not succeeded in staying at home for very long. He had already been sent to my father's brother, who was the abbot of a nearby monastery, and I did not see him.

. After the family had greeted me and made me feel very welcome, of course they wanted to know why I had run away from school. Looking back now, I don't know why I didn't say truthfully that I was homesick; the reason I gave was that I had broken a cup and had feared a punishment when this was discovered. Actually, this was not such a slight reason as it sounds, it was a serious matter for a child to break anything and so my parents accepted this explanation and no more was said.

It was decided that I could stay at the farm until my big brother's next visit. He came to the farm periodically to fetch supplies of meat, butter, cheese, fuel and so on to take back to Kundeling. I was relieved and very happy to hear I was not to be sent back immediately and after an enormous and very special supper (my first real meal for three days) I went to bed contented and slept soundly until late the next morning.

My mother decided I should continue my studies at home for the time being. She produced pens and paper and I sat on the porch to study. Well, sometimes I studied and sometimes I didn't! If I worked for half an hour before giving way to the temptation to run off and play that was very good and my mother was pleased!

I had not been at home long before Father decided to take me to see my young brother at the monastery about three hours ride away; I rode up in front of him—which seemed strange after riding my own pony in Kundeling, but I was happy to be riding with my father again.

When we arrived at the monastery I met my uncle, the abbot, for the first time. He was a very fat solemn man with a long luxurious beard, a mark of distinction in Tibet where bearded men are rare and the majority have no need to shave.

My young brother was now a monk and had started his religious studies, which at present consisted of learning prayers. Uncle asked me if I had learnt many prayers and I had to admit to only knowing one or two. He decided to have a competition between my young brother and me to see which one of us had learnt the most prayers. I did not like this idea at all, but there was no escape and my brother and I took it in turns to repeat a prayer we had learnt. It did not go very well. I was nervous and broke the prayer and was unable to continue. My brother had no trouble at all and won the 'competition' easily.

My father returned home the following day but I was to stay on at the monastery for a week. Father took one of my uncle's horses and left his own for me to ride home later. I was sorry to see him go and did not enjoy my week very much. At first my uncle made me say the prayer I broke over and over again and then he started to teach me more prayers. I could not concentrate on his teaching at all, I was always thinking of escaping outside to see if I could find someone to play with. But when I did succeed in this, there was no one about, everyone was busy memorizing their prayers and studying and my young brother had no time to play.

At last it was the end of the week and time for me to go home to Bhakar. My father's horse was brought round and I jumped into the saddle and set off for home. All I had to do was sit still; Father had left the horse behind for me deliberately, because it knew the way to the farm by itself.

It was late in the afternoon when we started for home and before long the sun set and the long twilight yielded to darkness. The horse loped gently along never missing a turning and I had nothing to do to occupy my thoughts. My mind began to fill with the stories of ghosts and spirits my big brother so often told me and fear clutched me as shadows seemed to dart across our path like black spirits. The wind had risen and the trees whispered and wailed wickedly. Once an owl screeched almost beside me and I nearly fell out of the saddle with terror. The horse was startled too and broke into a gallop. This fortunately put a momentary end to my fears, which had been close to panic; now I was having to give more thought to my riding—which was just as well. I was particularly afraid of owls because whenever I misbehaved at home, especially at night, my parents used to say, "If you are naughty the owl will come and take your ear."

The horse settled back into a gentle canter as we approached the farm, and the roar of the river rushing and dashing itself against the boulders sounded like the roar of a thousand angry spirits to my frightened imagination. I was immensely relieved when the horse at last brought me safely into our courtyard.

It was late and my father, becoming anxious, had been watching for us. He lifted me down from the saddle and hustled me into the house. I was very stiff with the cold and was glad to have my bowl of hot tuppa sitting snugly within the family circle round the great firepan which burned brightly, with the sweet scent of wood, in the centre of the room.

Mother was particularly relieved to see me. She had been very worried as it grew late and in her anxiety had consulted one of our shepherds, who had a great reputation as a soothsayer. He had prophesied from the rosary that I was quite safe and would be home soon. He was quite right. I arrived almost immediately afterwards!

As the days grew warmer I spent a good deal of my time in my newly discovered sport of horse racing.

My two friends and I would set out early in the morning to walk to a valley some distance away, where several farmers turned out their horses for summer grazing. The horses ran free, roaming the valleys and mountain slopes over quite a distance.

First of all we had to find some horses. This would sometimes take us all the morning. Then, having found them we must catch them and, clasping their manes firmly, half-swing and half-jump ourselves onto their bare backs. Immediately we would be away, racing pellmell across the fields at full gallop, often hurtling at an alarming speed down the steep green slopes of the mountains. I fell off several times during these hectic races, but I never hurt myself. It was all part of the fun.

Sometimes we found only one horse grazing quietly alone. Then we took turns for a gallop, or rode two at a time. Occasionally we could not find any horses at all and settled for oxen; but they were very slow compared with the horses and sometimes would not race at all but trotted slowly round and round in a circle. It was very dull. We soon tired of this and went home.

They were happy days, and homesickness and Kundeling were almost forgotten; but I knew it would not be long before my big brother came from Lhasa for the supplies and I would have to return with him for school again. I tried not to think about it.

7

THE ORACLE MAN

ONE day, shortly before my brother was expected to arrive from Kundeling, my uncle, the abbot, came to visit us for two or three days and give us news of my young brother's progress as a monk. He had ridden over from his monastery on a big blue roan horse which was turned loose on the mountains to graze during his visit.

At the end of his stay I was told to go and find his horse and bring it back to the farm. I walked quite a long way down the valley before I caught sight of it grazing high up the side of a bare mountain. As I drew closer I saw it had only a neck halter with no rope attached. This was disappointing; it was a big beautiful horse and I was very eager to ride it. After a moment's thought, I took off my chuba belt and put it in the horse's mouth as a bit and flung my chuba across its back for a saddle cloth. The horse was very tall, I was too small to mount it from the ground, so I led it to a hillock of grass to use as a mounting block and jumped onto its back.

Before I had time to gain my balance and get a good grip with my legs, the horse was off at full gallop down the grass mountain and I found I could not control it at all with my chuba belt 'bit'. As we sped downwards I slipped forward onto the horse's neck and felt myself falling. I grabbed its thick mane in an effort to save myself but it was no use and I was thrown heavily onto the ground. The horse stopped at once when I fell and stood quietly beside me. I got to my feet and tried to remount but found I could not lift my left arm, although it did not hurt at all. Every time I tried to lift it, my hand and forearm hung down loosely like a bell hammer. Fortunately we were now not far from home and I led the horse the rest of the way, my arm dangling oddly at my side but still without pain.

I took the horse to the stables to be saddled and went on into the house. I said nothing about my arm, although it was beginning to be very painful, and joined the family who were having a final cup of tea with my uncle before his departure. We had been sitting and chatting for quite a while when my father touched my left hand. I jumped so noticeably with the pain of it that I had to admit I had fallen and hurt my arm.

Everyone was immediately very concerned. My uncle, thinking I had probably dislocated my elbow, grasped my left hand and pulled with all his strength, thinking to straighten my arm. The pain was excruciating and I cried bitterly. No matter how hard uncle pulled he could not straighten my arm. At last he gave up the attempt and telling Father to put some jasang on it and tie it up with a cloth, he took his leave.

By now the pain in my arm was terrible and I could not sleep at all that night. Father and Mother tried to nurse me but they had no idea what to do. They decided that at first light Father would again take me to the nunnery inside the mountain a few miles behind our house.

The following morning my father carried me there on his back, and on our arrival one of the nuns, also thinking my arm was dislocated, pulled and pushed it vigorously, then rubbed it strenuously in an enthusiastic effort to straighten it. The pain of all this was quite agonizing and I could do nothing but scream and shout and cry with protest. At long last the nun mercifully gave it up, put on some jasang and sent me home.

Jasang was the cure for all ills and I had to eat some as well as having it spread on my arm!

I spent another wretched sleepless night. My arm was now so swollen it resembled a giant sausage; it seemed impossible that my skin could be stretched so tightly without bursting and I floated in a sea of throbbing pain.

At last the night came to an end and Father decided to take me to Drekung Medical College. He took me up in front on his horse, my arm was too painful for me to ride myself and we started off. The journey took a whole day and to me it seemed endless. The pain in my arm was agonizing, when we galloped it was jolted unbearably. I pleaded with my father to stop but all he said was "Be patient, it is not far now." I could see the hill on which the college stood in the distance and it never seemed to get any nearer. We arrived at last, just before sunset, the doctor saw us at once. He too thought my arm was dislocated and pulled and pushed it heartily. Next he examined the veins, then suddenly jerked my arm sharply towards him. I was almost beside myself with the pain of all this, and, looking back now, it is not really surprising, as I realize that my arm was not dislocated but broken.

All the doctor's efforts to straighten my arm came to nothing but a great deal of pain, and he finally said I must either stay at the medical college for two months or my father could nurse me at home under his, the doctor's, instructions. My father thought of leaving me at the college, but I cried and pleaded so fervently to go home with him that in the end he gave in.

The doctor gave him three or four different bottles of medicine and a special bottle of water to use to wash my arm before applying fresh jasang three times a day. There were also a number of other medicines of different colours to be taken at different times. My parents were going to be kept quite busy with all these medications!

Because of the long ride home, we stayed the night at the college planning an early start next day. Just before we left in the morning, the doctor washed my arm with some of the special water, which was ice-cold and painful. He then mixed some fresh jasang into a paste with the coloured medicines. This he spread thickly on my arm then wrapped it tightly with a bandage. This was how it was to be done three times a day when we got home.

The ride home was just as painful as before, but this time my father stopped for a rest every ten or fifteen minutes, which helped the pain a little but made it very late when we got home.

I didn't sleep that night, nor for many nights afterwards. By now my arm was so hugely swollen and painful I was forced to stay in bed. My parents meticulously carried out the doctor's instructions and applied fresh jasang paste and bandages three times a day. I dreaded these sessions, my arm was so tender that even the lightest touch felt like a hammer blow, and there did not seem to be any improvement. Finally my father decided to call the oracle man.

Once more the oracle consulted his holy ghost just as he had done when I cut my head falling off the goat, and once more the holy ghost gave my father the reason for my misfortune, through the medium of the oracle, and enjoined him to offer 100 butter lamps for my recovery. This the family did at once, but it was some time before my arm showed any noticeable improvement and several months before it could really be said to be healed. I don't know whether the jasang and the oracle man helped. Perhaps. But it was more than six months before I could bend my arm and very much longer than that before it was really well cured and free from pain.

The one thing that cheered me through all this was that, of course, it prevented me from returning to Kundeling and school. In spite of all the pain at least I was at home and with my parents.

Looking back now, I am glad I decided to play truant and run away home when I did. I am even glad I broke my arm and thus added months to my stay at home with my parents, because, as things turned out, I was never to see or have news of them again.

During this time, my brother made several visits to the farm for the supplies. His visits held no fears for me as long as my arm was swollen and useless, but finally the sad day dawned when it was decided that it was sufficiently healed for me to return to school (alas it was my left arm I had broken!), and after his next visit I unwillingly returned with my brother to Lhasa.

Our journey was uneventful. In spite of driving the six-in-hand, all strong spirited horses that needed skill and concentration, my brother never relaxed his watchfulness for a moment, quite rightly expecting me to seize the first opportunity to run back home.

Arrived in Lhasa, I had to go at once back to school in Norbulingka escorted firmly by my brother every foot of the way! I crept very unwillingly and was even more unhappy when I joined the class and found I had lost so much of my handwriting that I had to go back almost to the beginning and start again with Tupchen. I also had to write more lines every day than the other Tupchen writers, not only to regain my lost ground but as a punishment for running away.

I was not happy, I missed my home and parents very much. Although my life in Lhasa was more luxurious in the sense that city life is often more materially comfortable than that in the country, it was lonely; I missed the warmth and laughter in my home and the games with my friends. Here, everyone was kind but remote, absorbed in the all important business of learning and teaching. I disliked having to spend all my time in study and longed desperately for the carefree affectionate life of the farm.

I thought several times about running away again, but since my last escapade I was closely guarded at all times. No matter how I schemed, there was no opportunity; I was too well looked after!

In the end I decided I would just have to make the best of things as they were and I set myself to study hard in an effort to pass the time away.

8

PEACHES AND PORK

NOT long after my tenth Losar birthday His Holiness the Dalai Lama appointed my uncle to be Governor of Kongpo, a province in South-eastern Tibet. Sometimes called the Garden of Tibet, it covered an area roughly equivalent to the British Isles and was famous for, amongst other things, peaches, walnuts and walnut wood (for furniture) and pork.

Since my uncle was a *tsedrung* (monk) official this meant that a layman must also be appointed as government secretary. In the Tibetan government all government appointments must have both spiritual and secular representatives.

The journey to Tsela Dzong, the governor's residence, was to take three full days by 'bus', in reality a Chinese truck. My uncle, his older brother (the retired abbot) and the secretary went on ahead with two servants. I followed three days later with one of our cooks, the lay secretary's two sons and about fifteen other members of my uncle's staff and household.

Although we had a 'special luxury coach' (which meant that it was exactly the same as all the other Chinese trucks except that no members of the public were allowed to board it), there were no seats and we were rather overcrowded once we had all climbed aboard with all our luggage. We each had our Tibetan 'suitcase' with us. These are large long holdalls into which an enormous amount of clothing and belongings can be stuffed through the centre opening. Apart from their tremendous capacity, they are invaluable adjuncts to travel as they can either be opened out lengthwise as a mattress or rolled up to make a nice soft seat. So, thanks to our holdalls, we were not too uncomfortable, in spite of the plain wood flooring of the truck.

We set off from Kundeling about eight in the morning, and surprisingly soon afterwards arrived at Medoh Kongka, where we stopped for a short break. This was the border town of Drekung Province and I could see the way to my home. I felt terribly homesick and wanted desperately to run off and see my parents, but it was hopeless. I remembered my last visit to Medoh Kongka when I had slept the night in the haystall when I was running away home. I could see the house where I had been given shelter and I tried hard to think of a plan to slip away from the truck and perhaps hide in the haystall until dusk and then set out for home. But it was no good, we must go forward to Kongpo.

The first night we stopped at a village—well, hardly a village, there were only two houses and we slept in the truck. I did not sleep at all well. I was used to my nice room and comfortable bed, and in spite of my holdall mattress I tossed restlessly on the hard floor of the truck. I was not travel sick myself but many of the others had been quite ill on the drive and continued to be sick most of the night, which did not help me to sleep. When we resumed our journey at dawn the next day most of my fellow travellers were only half-conscious from travel sickness and headaches.

Accustomed to the comparatively slow speed of travelling on horseback, my first ever journey by truck seemed quite fast, and as the evening of this second day approached I could see that we had reached Upper Kongpo. Since we had left Medoh Kongka the road had climbed to the shoulder of the mountain range that ran due north, forming a natural boundary for Kongpo. The road twisted through the folded bare mountains, where the thick grass was dry and yellowed with the summer sun, crossing the pass at 20,000 feet and snow-free at this time of year. The road dropped sharply for the next 3,000 feet, corkscrewing round the steep slopes until it levelled itself into a twisting snake wrapped round the interlaced foothills, now

F

thickening with forest, until we rounded a particularly sharp bend and I saw the fertile plains of Kongpo stretching before us, framed on all sides by the distant mountain ranges spearing up into the sky. As we twisted down the mountainside the land became more and more thickly wooded. Firs and junipers gave place to towering rhododendron, walnuts, peach trees, flowering shrubs. Looking down from above the treeline, the lower slopes were so densely covered with the dark-green forest that the trees seemed to form a thick green counterpane flung carelessly across the shoulders of the hills. Soon we were swallowed by this lushness and the plain beyond was obscured. As our truck rattled past some particularly tall and beautiful rhododendron trees I wished we could stop for a moment and gather some sprays. We burn the sprays as incense, most especially when a member of the family is to undertake a journey; the incense from the sprays will ensure his safe journey.

As we came onto the plain, the sun was still high and the sky was a clear deep blue. It must have been late spring or early summer, because I remember the crops were quite high but still green, a jade-green sea rolling before the wind towards the distant mountains, punctuated with golden pools of mustard flowers, splashed across the fields like yellow paint on a Van Gogh canvas.

As the sun was setting we stopped at a place where the only building was a Chinese barracks. They could not accommodate us for the night and so once more we had to sleep in the truck. It was really most uncomfortable, but I was so dog-tired after the long drive and lack of sleep the night before, that once I at last fell asleep I slept soundly until dawn.

On this, the last day of our journey, we again left early, driving past many farms and villages and grove upon grove of the peach trees which grow wild and in great profusion in Kongpo. Presently, in the distance ahead, I caught the flash of water glinting in the brilliant sunlight and knew we must be nearing the Nyangchu River, with Nyitri, the end of the motor road, in the mountains beyond. We crossed the river in the late afternoon and not long afterwards arrived in Nyitri just as the sun went down.

We got down from the truck and I stood waiting, with our cook, for the traditional welcome to travellers. We stood for several minutes but nobody came. We were surprised. It was a small village and in addition there was a large Chinese barracks overlooking the road; we were sure our arrival could hardly have passed unnoticed. (Many years later I was to learn that the Chinese barracks had been empty. The Chinese had secretly tunnelled into the three mountains that surround Nyitri and fortified the tunnels in such a way that their troops could fire down directly onto the village and the road—as many Tibetan Freedom fighters were to find to their cost during the battles that took place after the uprising in 1959.)

Now we had come to the end of the motor road and must take to the more conventional form of Tibetan transport on horseback. It was the duty of every village to provide horses and food for official travellers (as a form of taxation) as far as the next village. But here we continued to wait and still nobody came, the village seemed deserted. Finally our cook decided to go in search of the person responsible for the food and transport and I was left alone at the truck.

I had not been standing alone many minutes when a man and a woman approached, the woman carried tea and pancakes which she offered to me. She was bent and wrinkled with age and addressed me in the Kongpo dialect, which I did not understand at all. I was about to accept the proffered food when I remembered that before leaving Lhasa I had been warned about the Kongpo people's belief that if they poisoned people of higher families they would inherit their spirits, and told never to accept any food in Kongpo unless I was sure it was safely free from poison. I quickly changed my mind and shook my head rather regretfully; I was very hungry and the pancakes looked delicious! Seeing me reluctantly refusing the food, the old man realized my suspicions and at once assured me, in Central Tibetan dialect which he spoke quite well, that they had no intention of trying to poison me, to prove his point he ate a little of the food himself. Reassured, I tucked into the snack and was just finishing the last pancake when our cook returned with the horses and a groom and we went off to spend the night with the village headman, who was a wealthy land-owner and had a large comfortable house. He had many horses, cows, chickens and black pigs, and was, I suppose, what the West would call a dairy farmer. Kongpo cows are not unlike Western cattle in appearance and give a great deal of rich creamy milk—we did not breed cattle for beef as only the very poor people would eat it. Kongpo pork was renowned for its succulence—peaches grow in such profusion in the province that pigs and cattle were encouraged to feed on the heavy wind-falls in the orchards—and of course wild peaches and many other fruits were there for the eating.

After a very comfortable night and some really good food I felt quite refreshed when we set off the next morning to ride the rest of the way to Tsela Dzong.

I little thought as I said good-bye to this kind family (Mr and Mrs Lawang) that we would meet again in very different circumstances on our flight from the Chinese.

Almost immediately after leaving the Lawangs we had to re-cross the Nyangchu River, only this time there was no bridge and we piled into yak-skin boats with the horses swimming alongside. Once across we rode on for half a day. It need not have taken so long, but we had to change our horses at every village and this took time. The horses were only provided from one village to the next. Sometimes we got good horses but at others they were poor-looking things and very slow.

The country through which we were now riding was very beautiful. Kongpo was fertile and prosperous; as well as peaches and other fruits, there are innumerable walnut trees, the wood of which was in great demand for furniture and the nuts, sent mainly to Lhasa. The nuts are particularly large, and many shepherds and travellers use the shells to carry butter, which they smear on their faces to protect their skin from the wild winds that so often blow cold and vigorously at such altitude —14,000 and 15,000 feet above sea level. The green outer shells of the nuts are made into green dye, often used to enhance the very beautiful shoes for which Kongpo is justly renowned.

As we rode across the plain with the Nyangchu tumbling northwards to our left, the mountains on our right gradually tapered and were halted by the Nyangchu where it forked to join the Tsangpo. Kongpo people saw this range as an elephant lying asleep with its trunk outstretched towards the junction of the two rivers. Poised on the tip of the trunk stood Tsela Dzong, with a panoramic view of the central plain, a green and gold carpet laid serenely to the feet of the blue mountains framing the horizon and the two rivers forming a foaming, fast-running natural moat 1,000 feet below.

Tzong is the Tibetan word for castle or fortress and Tsela Dzong, as the official residence of the Governor, was not only the private residence but also contained all the government offices. Enclosed within its thick high walls were the paraphernalia of administration, the law courts, the prison, stables and huge stores. The governor was also the judge for the province, which was divided into Upper and Lower Kongpo and sub-divided into districts each of which was administered by an official answerable to the governor. There were no radio or telephone communications and the only road the one we travelled from Lhasa to Nyitri, and even this journey by truck took over three days; it was impossible to keep in touch with Lhasa and the central government. The general government policies were known before leaving Lhasa but once arrived in Kongpo the governor was very much on his own and decisions and justice were his alone.

Tsela Dzong was an almost entirely new building—most of the old one had been destroyed by an earthquake a few years before. It had been rebuilt with huge blocks of stone, the outside walls unpainted but very beautiful because the stone had a natural variegation of blue and pink tones with the delicate shading of a water colour. When we rode into the courtyard, however, the inner walls shone with spotless white paint.

My uncle had already arrived, but the outgoing Governor was staying on for two weeks to hand over the keys and explain the current business and so on. He was of course still in the governor's residence, which was in the old part of the Dzong untouched by the earthquake; so we were housed temporarily in the new building. Our rooms here were enormous and very cold, this was probably because they were new and the stone walls and floors were not as warm as the bricks of the old building. I shared a vast room with my very old uncle, the retired abbot and it was freezing.

Kongpo people used to say that Tsela Dzong was the coldest, noisiest place in the whole of Kongpo. Strategically it was superbly placed, perched as it was at the end of the mountain range with an uninterrupted view of the surrounding country on all three sides and the rising mountain range for protection at its back; but climatically it was also unprotected from the strong and almost constant wind that raged and howled about the mountain, in its wilder moments rising to a piercing scream as it tore its way through the cracks of the tall flag pole which stood like a ship's mast atop the battlements. To this day the most evocative sound of all is howling wind. But it seemed very safe, perched up there overlooking the plains for hundreds of miles, the mountains rising securely at our back and the rushing rivers moated below. Alas how wrong this feeling of security turned out to be and how strategically tempting we were. But this was the future, the present was cold, noisy but very beautiful.

Two days after we arrived, in accordance with custom, the people came to welcome their new Konchi, my uncle, bringing offerings of every kind.

Kongpo is one of the largest Provinces in Tibet and some of the people had travelled for many days to bring their greetings. From every corner of the province came the headman of each village and several villagers until there was quite a multitude of people gathered in and around the Dzong. Everyone wore their best clothes and it was a good opportunity to see how different the Kongpo people were from the Central Tibetans; not only in their dialect, which I could not understand at all, but also in their clothes. Over their chubas they wore leotards, sometimes in fine wool like vicuna and trimmed with an abundance of colourful embroidery; but more often in the colder weather and for travelling the leotards for both the men and the women were made of skin; the poorer people used the pretty grey fur of monkeys, but the wealthier ones wore leopard, mink, or the most exclusive, gyalpak, a very beautiful but expensive pale fawn skin of a deer family rare in Tibet, a small gazelle-like creature with long black horns. The women, who have a reputation for beauty, encircle their leotards with finely worked silver or gold belts and their hats and shoes are exquisitely embroidered with lavishly colourful designs.

As Central Tibetans, we did not wear leotards; our chubas were very warm, everything—even the fine wool shirts which we wore under our chubas—was completely lined with lamb-skin. We had sheepskins on our beds, and like all children, I had a sheepskin sleeping bag.

Every Kongpo man over the age of 15 carries a sword, many of these are very beautifully inscribed with traditional designs on the blade and silver, or gold and jewelled decorations on the leather scabbard. Most of these swords have been handed down from father to son for generations and are hundreds of years old; the blades are kept as shining and sharp as if they had been forged yesterday and are by no means carried purely for dress and decoration; they are a businesslike part of the Kongpo man's every day life and are very often the family's most treasured possession. The owner means what he says when he declares he would sooner die than be parted from his sword—a truth that the Chinese underestimated when they presently demanded that all Tibetans must hand over their weapons to their nearest Chinese official; the immediate Kongpo reaction was 'Take our swords if you dare' and many a fierce battle ensued. But when we arrived in Kongpo the Chinese were still trying to coerce and cajole us into accepting our 'liberation'.

The Kongpo welcome to my uncle went on for several days and during the offerings one of the Kongpo presented me with a pair of beautiful Kongpo boots. The toes were of very fine blue leather, the lower part of the shoe above the thick sole consisted of three thicknesses of white wool quilted and embroidered with silks, the upper part of the shoe was red velvet and the leg pure pink wool. They were quite beautiful and I was delighted with them.

Unfortunately they were too big for me and it was six months before I could wear them.

9

AT THE CAVE OF THE KING

A T the end of two weeks, the outgoing minister left Tsela Dzong and we moved into the private residence. It was a very old building constructed of weathered brick which had withstood the earthquake and was much warmer and not so vast; but the rooms were spacious and well proportioned. The house was almost entirely surrounded by a garden, which was laid out so that it caught the sun almost all day and was sheltered from the ever-present wind by a high wall. In the warm sheltered sunshine the flowers grew in colourful profusion and I found it an excellent place to sunbathe, watching the birds and feasting on the myriad colours and scents about me.

My uncle soon found me a teacher—an elderly Kongpo, well educated and good in Tibetan grammar—and I had my lessons in the garden.

It was rather lonely. I had to spend a great deal of my time in study and in my brief free time I had to behave myself. It was my uncle's wish that I should not mix with the local children; as I was the only child at the Dzong this meant that I had no companions, but I was not allowed to play very much in any case, I had to concentrate on my studies. It was very difficult to get permission to go swimming or on a picnic, my uncle would say "You must finish your studies first" and usually by the time I had finished them it was too late to go.

Sometimes in the evenings I accompanied the servants when

they led the horses down to drink, riding one of the horses bareback down to the river. My uncle did not approve of me doing
this and finally it was forbidden. My own pony had not yet
arrived; it was coming with my brother who was bringing the
rest of our horses and mules from Lhasa.

My daily routine seldom varied. My lessons started at half
past eight in the morning and continued to half past four, then,
if I did not have too much homework, I sometimes had time for
a short walk before supper at six. After supper, I had to stay
beside my uncle, listening to the conversation until he sent me
to bed, usually about eight.

My room was small but nice and warm, with polished wooden
walls like a log cabin. The window was unglazed and covered
with fine net so that I could see out but no one could see in.
There were two beds, one for my brother when he arrived from
Lhasa later. I had a small walnut table with an oil lamp and this
completed the furnishings.

My brother finally arrived after we had been at the Dzong
for three months. Although he was fifteen years older than I,
I was very pleased to see him—we had become quite good companions; but most particularly I was delighted to be reunited
with my pony which he had brought with him. Although I was
not allowed to ride her very often except when I accompanied
my uncle on his official visits through the province, I used to
creep into the kitchens and beg carrots and other titbits from
the cooks to take to the stables for her after lessons were over
for the day.

My brother slept in my room and I no longer felt so lonely.
He was good company and used to tell me stories, although
sometimes they were ghost stories which frightened me and kept
me awake in terror long after my brother had fallen asleep.
Sometimes he would tell me there was a ghost standing by my
bed. Shuddering with dread, I cowered under my sheepskin
covers, terrified to move or even breathe.

My bedtime stories were not always ghostly; my brother also
had an endless fund of fairy tales, ancient Tibetan stories told
round family firesides for generations. He had very little to do

at Tsela Dzong, so when my uncle sent me to bed he would often come to my room with me and spin a story. He enjoyed telling them and just carried on talking even if I stopped listening or fell asleep before the end.

Occasionally my daily routine was interrupted by a visit to a place of interest or, more rarely, I accompanied my uncle on his round of official visits. There were many places of historical interest on the mountains.

I particularly remember a visit to the cave of Gyalpo Timmi Kundun, one of the kings of Tibet, who is reputed to have spent nearly all his life in this cave. It was on our mountain just above the Dzong, so we went on foot, taking our lunch with us.

After a steep climb we reached a small waterfall, just before the cave. The falls were high but not wide and the water fell like smoke onto a beehive-shaped stone below.

Legend demanded that before anyone visited the cave, they must strip, wash themselves in the falls and circle the hive-shaped stone three times to be completely cleansed physically and spiritually before entering the cave.

The last man round the stone this day was the one-eyed servant of the General Secretary. With some agitation he told us that on his way round he had seen the body of a dead black dog; none of us had seen it and we were afraid it must mean bad luck for him so he was not allowed to come to the cave with us. My uncle explained to him that no one was allowed to visit the cave if they had seen a bad omen on the way. Of course there were good signs too, particularly anything white, and white storks abounded and were often seen. Leaving the man beside the waterfall we continued our climb to the cave. We could see the entrance almost directly above us but the way was very steep and difficult. At last we arrived and I was surprised and a little disappointed to see how small it was. It contained a tiny fireplace, perhaps where he made his food and a small mat where he sat, these and a small statue of King Timmi Kundun himself, erected by the people after his death, were all there was to see inside the cave. Indeed there was no room for anything else it was so small. Both the fireplace and the mat were in very good repair. I think they must have been put there by the people and replaced periodically to give an idea of how it looked when the King lived there; otherwise certainly the mat would have been rotten after so many years.

Coming out of the cave, we climbed down a short distance to a tree shaped like an umbrella where legend says the King used to rest. We also decided to have a short rest. It was a perfect day, the sun hot and shining brilliantly, we were sheltered from the wind which blew on the other side of the mountain. The air was transparently clear and in the infinite stillness we could see the blue ribbon of rivers far below us threading through the fields and past the many villages scattered across the plain to the feet of the mountains blue and purple on the horizon.

It was cool and peaceful resting under the tree. Almost beside me, under the tree, was a small square stone on which there was a print of King Timmi Kundun's 'bottom', two 'seat' marks as it were, so we can say, "he sat here."

Timmi Kundun was a king who was famous for his generosity and there are many legends about him and his unselfishness. Through the years some of these stories have become rather exaggerated in the telling—some of the legends say that he even gave away his eyes—but perhaps these stories are told as parables only. Anyway, it is a fact that he was so generous in giving his material possessions to those in need that in the end he had nothing but the small mat and the cooking pot that we saw in the cave.

Many people make a pilgrimage to this cave, particularly on special holidays. For many of them the compulsory cleansing in the waterfall before entering the cave is almost as much an unusual experience as the pilgrimage itself as not everyone has the opportunity (or the taste) for a daily submersion in glacial mountain water, which is the sole choice if you are travelling or have no settled home.

The sun was setting and it was beginning to get cold under

the tree so we set off for home, and by the time we got back I was glad of a good supper and quite ready for bed.

Some weeks later, I remember, we made quite a long journey to the Dhemo Monastery. Here, every four years they have a Lama Dance, and we were invited to this.

It took two days on horseback and all the way from Tsela Dzong the people of the villages had heard the *Konchi* was coming and they had arranged receptions.

First of all we crossed the river at the foot of our mountain. There were no bridges; we crossed in yak-skin boats. The river is not very wide but the current is extremely strong; in order to reach the correct spot on the other bank, the boatmen had to start out high up-river on the near bank and the current swept up downwards and across with a great rush. It needed great skill on the part of the boatmen to guide us through the rushing waters and prevent us overturning. The boatmen know the rivers in every mood, the job is handed down from father to son for generations. Quite often the man is accompanied by a tame sheep, loaded with his gear and food. The sheep follows the boatman, like Mary in the nursery rhyme, wherever he goes. Legend says that a high family decided to slaughter a sheep and the particular sheep selected happened to be pregnant. They left her in the fold with the other sheep with orders to their servant to send for the butcher the following day. That night, the shepherd, who slept in a shelter in the corner of the sheep fold, overheard the sheep talking to one another, as the condemned sheep gave birth to her lamb. The sheep gave advice to her new lamb "not to go in front of the flock because wolves might attack the flock and the ones in the front would be the first to be attacked; don't go at the end of the flock because the shepherd might shoot his catapult and the stone might hit the lamb and break its leg; so, said Mother sheep, always go in the middle of the flock!" Hearing all this, the shepherd was struck with sorrow at the thought of the little newborn lamb being left an unprotected orphan and by the mother sheep's anxiety for its safety when she was no longer there to protect it, that he decided to take both the sheep and its lamb away and they all ran off into the mountains, until they came to a lake and met a fisherman. The fisherman had caught a big golden fish. The shepherd asked the fisherman not to kill the fish, but the fisherman refused; he wanted it for his supper he said. Then the shepherd told the fisherman that if he would return the fish to the water and promise not to fish any more, the shepherd would give him the sheep and the lamb, but of course he must promise not to kill them. The fisherman was quite pleased with this idea, because the sheep was sturdy enough to carry the fisherman's bags and her coat was thick and would provide warm wool. Of course, now he had given his word to the shepherd that he would not fish anymore, or take life in any form, he had to find some other way to make a living and since he knew the lakes and rivers of his district very well he decided to become a boatman. He made himself a yak-skin corracle and was soon in business, followed everywhere he went by his sheep and her lamb. So legend explains why it is that so many Tibetan boatmen are always accompanied by a pet sheep carrying their packs. The legend of the shepherd goes on through many adventures and he is ultimately rewarded for his acts of kindness and compassion in saving many lives by being transported to Nymph Land and presented with a magic lotus. But that is another story.

But to get back to our river crossing. When we reached the opposite bank, we left the boats and mounted our horses, who were rather wet, as they had crossed the river alone swimming alongside the boats. Almost at once we reached the town of Nyago-Lupting, spread at the foot of the mountain ahead of us. The people had put up a large, beautifully embroidered tent on a wide grass plain between the river and the mountains, just outside the town. As we were ushered into the tent I noticed how colourful the furnishings looked with the splendid carpets and shining walnut table carved with intricate designs. Everywhere we went throughout the province on my uncle's official visits magnificent ceremonial tents were erected and it was a point of honour with each town or village to furnish the interior as beautifully as possible. The reception was always more or less the same. First of all my uncle spent about an hour receiving the people of the area, none of whom came empty handed as this would have been the height of rudeness and disrespect. They brought offerings dictated by tradition, cups of chang, rice and troma. Troma is a root that grows underground and when cooked tastes very sweet and a little like coconut. The leaves are a delicate silver-grey and grow along the surface of the earth instead of upwards like most plants. Troma is traditionally symbolic of good luck, 'Tro' is phonetically the same as tro meaning luck. White scarves accompanied all these offerings. These are always given or exchanged as a form of greeting; the colour white represents goodness and good fortune and the presentation of a white scarf infers that you wish these blessings on your friend; they are also a mark of respect and are always presented to senior officials on formal occasions, as well as friends and family members who are to make or have come on a long journey far away from home.

Fortunately it was not the custom to eat and drink all the offerings, which were in any case only brought in token quantities; it was sufficient to take only a tiny portion from each bowl. It would be an impossibility to take all that was offered—especially in Kongpo, which was one of the most densely populated areas of Tibet—because on our way to each new reception the people of the countryside came from their houses and offered food and chang to us as we passed along the way.

After the ceremony of the offerings was completed, there was a short entertainment. Usually the boys and girls performed some Kongpo dances accompanied by singing and dan-yen (Tibetan guitar) playing. This sort of ceremony was repeated throughout our tour.

One of our calls was the village of Tchujoh, which is very well-known throughout Tibet because of the legend concerning the village well, from which the village derives its name. (Tchu meaning water; Joh meaning Lord Buddha.)

A peasant from Kongpo went to Lhasa to the Temple of Johkang. Inside the temple he saw for the first time the gigantic golden image of Joh. Legend says that the peasant asked the Joh to look after one of his shoes while he went shopping. A loud voice from somewhere high above him said, "Yes," he would look after the shoe and the peasant, well satisfied, went off into Lhasa to make his purchases. When he returned to the temple for his shoe, he thanked the Joh for looking after it and invited him to visit his house in Kongpo. The Joh accepted his invitation. The peasant was delighted and returned to his house in Kongpo and told his wife all about the incident and the Joh's promise to come and visit them. They kept a very watchful eye for this visit for some time, and after a while the peasant's wife saw the Joh in the well when she went to draw some water. Greatly excited she rushed back to her husband and told him what she had seen. He immediately hurried out to the well to see for himself and looking down the well saw that it was indeed the Joh who had accepted his invitation. He at once asked him to come into the house, but the Joh would not accept this invitation saying that he could not go over the peasant's doorstep, and so saying he disappeared from the well. The peasant told everyone about the Joh in his well and the story spread all over Tibet. And from that day everyone tries to visit this well, especially pilgrims, and anyone who is lucky can see the Joh in the well. We all looked down the well but none of us saw the Joh. We were very unlucky!

We also visited the peasant's house, where his descendants still live. My chief impression was that it was rather an old looking house.

We arrived at Dhemo Monastery just as the sun was setting and were made very welcome by the abbot and the minister of Dhemo district who was also there to greet us. It was not very long after this meeting that the Dhemo minister was arrested by the Red Chinese, handcuffed and led away to oblivion; but no shadow of this fell across our visit at this time and after a very good supper I went off to bed and slept soundly after the excitement and travel of the past two days.

Dhemo Monastery contained about 600 monks and the following day was spent seeing all the temples, where we offered butter lamps at the many altars, and then we visited the different groups in the monastery. All monasteries of any size in Tibet were comprised of different 'houses', in much the same way as a Western university is composed of different colleges. The groups in the monastery were more or less self-contained within the monastery, and just as a university college may gain a reputation for excelling in the classics or sport by virtue of oustanding professors in these subjects, so the monastic groups within their houses might individually achieve a reputation for excellence in a particular subject such as art or music or classical religious studies because the particular teachers in that group happened to be especially gifted in these fields.

The following day we all got ready to see the Lama Dances. The dancing was to take place in a large courtyard. A high platform had been prepared for us and many other guests, who included the Dhemo minister, the abbot, the high lamas of the monastery and some Chinese officers from the barracks at Nyitri. The Chinese always sent representatives to any occasion where they knew there would be many Tibetans attending. It was the only opportunity they had of spreading their Communist propaganda to the country people gathered together in one place.

We had a very good view from our platform and I could see not only the dancers but all the Tibetans in their best clothes crowded round the sides of the courtyard. Many of them had come from villages and farms many miles from the monastery and I felt sorry to notice that some of them could see very little of the dancing because there were so many people trying to watch.

Lama dances are a traditional interpretation of religious history and the characters are recognizable by the costumes and masks that they wear. The story unfolds like a classical ballet. The music is limited to the instruments customarily played in monasteries; that is to say there are no stringed instruments such as the dan-yen. There is a strict division between instruments played by the monks for religious ceremonies and instruments played by laymen for ordinary singing and dancing. The monks play a variety of wind instruments that include a

G

very long horn, that produces deep bass notes; another that
resembles a seventeenth-century clarinet and a third which is
not unlike a short post horn. The 'clarinet' is made of wood
and decorated in silver and gold. The long and short horns are
copper and trimmed with silver, or occasionally made entirely
from silver. Then there are a variety of drums, cymbals and
bells. The monk musicians are professionals and it takes many
years to become expert in the art of blowing the music. The
long horn or doong requires long practice to achieve the necessary lip vibrations and prolonged breaths required to produce
an admirable sustained tone, and the players practice for hours
every day before they become proficient. The smaller horns,
the qyalin and peewang, do not involve the difficult lip vibrations but breathing needs a great deal of practice, because, like
the Western oboe player, these horn players must learn to take
in breath through their noses simultaneously with blowing it
out through their mouths to make a sound without the smallest
pause.

At last the dances began. The costumes were gorgeous, made
from the very finest silks and brocades in Tibet and full of rich-
ness and colour. Each colour was appropriate to the character
played by the dancer so that he was immediately recognized,
for example Death was always symbolized by a skeleton in-
variably dressed in a tightly fitting costume of scarlet with the
ribs and other bones painted in white.

It was a pageant of illustrated history spread before us for
our enjoyment and many of the dances had been performed constantly for hundreds of years. To me, one of the most exciting
chapters was the dance that tells the story of how the Black
Hat overcame King Langtama in the tenth century. I had heard
this story very often and perhaps I enjoyed this dance the most
because I was particularly familiar with this story.

Well over 1,000 years ago King Lha-Tho-Tho-ri introduced
Buddhism into Tibet and the religion flourished and spread
throughout the country until the tenth century when King
Langtama came to the throne. He was a sinful man who
systematically set about to destroy religion in Tibet. The story

tells of the country left without religion and all the lamas assassinated but one. This one remaining was a High Lama who resolved to restore religion to the people and devised a scheme to rid them of the irreligious king. He dyed his monk robes black and carefully painted his white horse with the same black dye. When all was ready, he hid a bow and some arrows in long sleeves of his robes and rode off to see the king, planning to kill him and then to revive religion. The king, not realizing he was a high lama, received him in the courtyard of the palace and the lama offered to dance for him. This pleased the king. The lama started his dance then suddenly took his bow and arrow and shot the king. As he fell dead to the ground the lama quickly leapt on to his waiting horse and galloped away towards the river, pursued by the king's guards. While the guards were still some distance behind, horse and lama plunged into the river Kyichu and swam across to the other side. During their swim the rushing waters of the river had washed away the dye both from the lama's robes and from the horse so that by the time the guards reached the river bank all they could see was a red-robed lama riding quietly by on a white horse along the opposite side of the river. No sign whatever of the Black Hat on the black horse who had just killed the king. So Buddhism was revived in Tibet.

The Lama Dances went on for two days and I thoroughly enjoyed them all. At the end of the final dance the Chinese arranged a film show. This was of course the reason for their presence at the monastery; this was their chance to show their communist propaganda films to a large gathering of Tibetans who were normally too isolated to be reached by such things.

I could not follow the film at all. There were a lot of Chinese marching about cheering and waving flags and generally trying to show how marvellous communism was. The Tibetans did not like it at all. They were particularly displeased to hear the communists in the film speak out against religion, but nothing was said to the Chinese who showed the film because the Tibetans were still trying to tolerate the invaders and the revolution had not yet begun. All the same the Tibetans made their displeasure quite obvious to the Chinese in an unobtrusive manner.

On our way back to Tsela Dzong the following day we were invited to stay with someone who was reputed to be the richest man in Kongpo (many people said he was the richest man in Tibet). He certainly had a huge and quite magnificent house and so many horses and mules that he had never counted them and let many of them run wild, with the result that many of them were less than half-broken for riding. This fact aroused considerable fun the next day, when the village arranged a sports display for us. One of the events involved catching and trying to ride some of the untamed horses. There were many volunteers for this event and some of the men were successful but quite a few of them fell off and hurt themselves.

We left the next morning and went to the monastery at Chamnag, not far from Tsela Dzong—in fact I could see the Dzong on the other side of the river from Chamnag Monastery. The Minister of Chamnag District was there to receive us and there were many Tibetans from the outlying villages of the district to welcome us with scarves. It was to be not many months later that this District Minister scrambled through the night in nothing more than the clothes he stood up in and reached Tsela Dzong just in time to join us in our headlong flight from the Chinese; but today there were no such clouds in the sky and we stayed there peacefully for the night.

Chamnag was being rebuilt and was not quite completed. There had been a big monastery on the same site, but it had been destroyed entirely in the earthquake that had also destroyed part of Tsela Dzong a few years before.

After a good supper, my uncle settled down to an evening of Mahjong, a game I was never allowed to watch so I went off to bed.

The following morning we went round the buildings and the gardens and then crossed the river and back to Tsela Dzong.

10

RIDING THROUGH THE NIGHT

LIFE continued peacefully enough in the Dzong, but I noticed that the officers from the Chinese barracks 12 miles away called more frequently for meetings with my uncle and each time they were more stern and unsmiling. Rumours began to reach us of villages in other districts destroyed and looted and the children kidnapped and sent to school in China. It became increasingly obvious that the Chinese policy of friendly persuasion was giving place to a far tougher line of brute force and insistence on the Tibetan's acceptance of communism. The Tibetans were equally determined not to become communists. It became a case of an irresistible force meeting an immovable object and the resulting impasse exploded into open revolt by the Tibetans against their oppressors.

On 10th March 1959 Tibetans in Lhasa, fearing for the safety of His Holiness the Dalai Lama and exasperated by the bullying duplicity of the communists, hurled themselves into an attack which was incredible for its fearlessness and courage but was doomed to fail in the face of superior Chinese weapons and trained soldiery. Nevertheless, the uprising was the signal for fighting to commence throughout Tibet and the men grabbed their swords and a few Lee Enfield rifles and flung themselves against the Goliath that was trampling their country to death.

We knew nothing of what was happening in Lhasa, and so it was that when the shouted warning of approaching Chinese dragged us from our beds in the middle of the night my uncle assumed the attack would come from the east. We were making

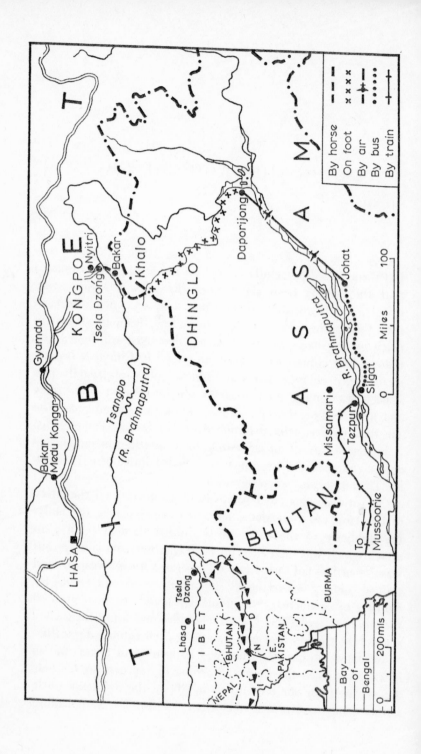

for Lhasa and the Pota-la when I found myself dozing on a hillock and dreaming of home.

It was sunset and time for me to be getting back to the house. I had heard my uncle tell our host that we must continue our flight to Lhasa in the morning.

I slept fitfully that night and was glad when dawn came and we said good-bye to our host and rode on our way.

We had soon passed the forest land and the countryside was now much more open, with bare (green grass) mountains. We became alarmed lest the Chinese caught up with us; my uncle would be a very prize catch for them. There were very few villages now and we had to camp by the roadside feeling horribly exposed and unprotected. Fortunately it was not very cold. Evenings in Tibet are generally mild, it is the dawn that is the really cold time until the sun comes over the mountains to warm the day. Early the next morning we made our breakfast by the roadside before setting off again towards Lhasa.

As we rode on we began to pass a little snow, but we made good speed until about noon when we came to the foot of a snow mountain; it was not as steep as many Tibetan mountains but we could see some other travellers in the distance above us having a very difficult time to get through the snow, we decided to have our lunch before tackling the climb ourselves.

There were no streams nearby so our cook collected half a pot of snow which he boiled for our tea and tsampa. Warmed and fortified by this lunch, we started climbing. The sun shone brilliantly and the glare from the snow hurt my eyes. Most of our party were wearing a welding-type goggles, very popular with travellers. I had nothing of the kind and managed as best I could by keeping my eyes almost closed and pulling my hat well down to cover them, trusting to my pony to find the best route up the mountain.

To begin with the snow was not very deep and we tried to follow the trail made by the travellers ahead of us. But it was difficult; there was a high wind and the snow was constantly drifting.

At one point my brother's horse suddenly sank up to its

belly in deep snow. It must have stepped into a drift or a small mountain pit. The more it struggled to lift its legs clear of the snow the deeper it sank. Everyone dismounted and started to shovel the deep snow aside. It took a long time, we had to be careful not to land in the pit ourselves, but at last the horse was able to lift its feet clear of the snow that imprisoned it and move forward. We finally reached the further side of the mountain and at the end of the snow path there was a small village where some other travellers were already having a meal. They told us that they too were on their way to Lhasa in a bid to escape the Chinese. We had already had our lunch, so we just had a short rest before riding on again.

It had taken longer to cross the mountain than we thought and we had to ride fast to reach another village before dark. It was already getting late, but the way was comfortable and easy and we reached the village in good time without any trouble. But then we found it was impossible to find a house where we could stay the night. The village was completely full of travellers, also running to Lhasa, who had arrived ahead of us.

Eventually one of the villagers took us to a small nearby monastery where they gave us comfortable accommodation and a good supper. The next morning my uncle went to see one of the High Lamas of the monastery to ask if there would be any difficulties on our way to Lhasa. The Lama told him that conditions were certainly very bad; he had heard that there were many Chinese soldiers ready for action and that Tibetans were joining the Tibetan army in large numbers and forming themselves into guerilla groups to attack the Chinese when and where they could. He thought that by the very roundabout route that we were taking it would be possible to reach Lhasa, but the main route through Nyitri was out of the question, it would be impossible for us to evade capture if we went that way.

Obviously we would have to continue on this long cross-country route we had taken if we were to reach Lhasa safely.

We rode off just after breakfast the next day. We had many more snow mountains to cross and it was now very much colder. For much of the way we were well above the snowline and some of the passes were over 20,000 feet high. The strong winds drifted the snow across our path and into our faces and at times we were enveloped in thick wet cloud. It was very slow and uncomfortable but at last we descended into the foothills again and came to a big river which must be crossed by boat. The boat was made of a huge log hollowed out in the centre. The horses and mules could swim across but first their packs and saddles must be taken off and loaded into the boat. It took the boat three trips to ferry all our things across but at last we were all on the other side. We reloaded the mules, saddled our horses and rode on.

We had nothing to eat that day until we camped at sunset. There was another big river in front of us and on the opposite bank we could see two nomad tents.

We had our supper quickly and were soon in bed, ready for an early start the next day.

Very late in the night we were awakened by the sound of galloping horses. It was a dark night, we had no fire and could see nothing. We kept quiet, almost holding our breath as the pounding horses approached. We were very afraid that they were Chinese, but as they drew nearer we could hear them speaking Tibetan. Very relieved we shouted to them to come over to talk to us.

They were Kongpo volunteer soldiers and were coming from a fight with the Chinese that had taken place at Chumna, not far from Tsela Dzong and they told us the Chinese were still hesitating to attack Tsela Dzong, believing it was strongly manned and fortified against them. Years later I heard that Tsela Dzong had been captured by the Chinese almost a week after this battle of Chumna and ten days after we had so hastily left in the middle of the night.

The soldiers went on to tell us that the Dhemo District Minister had been arrested and led away in handcuffs, and we realized from this that Dhemo District must have been con-

quered. They warned us that there was a detachment of Chinese
soldiers not far from our camp and riding towards us. On hearing this, we rushed to get everything ready to move on at
once. There was no moon and it was difficult to load everything
onto the mules in the pitch dark. We were unable to see what
we were doing and in our hurry my brother took my saddle by
mistake, I was left with a saddle much too large for my pony,
which was very uncomfortable for both of us, but it was useless
to try to change over and in any case there was no time. I had
to make the best of it and we rode on very fast.

Soon we found ourselves riding along an empty river bed
full of rocks and shingle which the horses found very difficult.
There was no other way to go. There were mountains on our
right and impenetrable bushes and thorn shrubs on our left so
the horses were forced to stumble and slide along the river bed
as best they could. Our progress made a great noise and we were
terrified the Chinese would hear us. We would most certainly
be trapped in such surroundings, but there was nothing to be
done but to go forward. At last the banks began to open out
into a plain and we could leave the river bed and ride silently
and swiftly.

It was still very dark but the plain made our progress easy
and presently the sky began to lighten in the east and dawn
came. As the light spread up the sky we had to start climbing
again, but this time it was a bare mountain with no snow to
impede us.

Half-way up the mountainside, we met about twenty Khamba
soldiers coming towards us from Lhasa. They told us Lhasa had
been taken by the Chinese after some brief but very fierce fighting. They said many Tibetans were fleeing towards India. The
Khambas' horses were very tired and weak; they had been
ridden hard for a long way and the Khambas demanded that we
exchange our good horses for their worn-out ones. They said
they were going to continue to fight for our country and we
must give them our horses if we were not joining them in the
fighting. My uncle agreed—he had no choice. The Khambas,
fiercely independent and militant by nature, said they would

shoot us if we refused, and we did not doubt that they meant what they said.

I was heartbroken to have to part with my pony and have wondered many times since what became of her. The Khambas' horses were very weak and exhausted and in place of my beloved sturdy little roan I got a tall white skinny horse. The poor thing was so weak and tired it could hardly walk, its ears floated down the sides of its face in utter dejection.

The Khambas also demanded one of our pack mules and in return gave us one of theirs. We had no sooner loaded it with a pack than it fell over and rolled down the mountain, together with its pack. It plummeted over and over and when at last it rolled to a stop against a rock far below we could see that the poor thing was already dead. We did not want to waste any more time climbing down to retrieve the pack—it was a long way down and very steep—so we simply abandoned it.

So we rode along on those poor horses. The Khambas' news that Lhasa had fallen into the hands of the Chinese made us realize it was useless to continue our journey towards the city; but we could not go back either, the Chinese were still close behind us and in possession of Tsela Dzong. We had no choice but to try to find our way to India. Although we could now only ride very slowly because of the exhausted condition of the horses, even this snail's pace soon proved too much for my poor white horse. It collapsed and threw me onto the ground. Fortunately I did not hurt myself, but I felt very sorry for the horse. It seemed to have passed out altogether, but we could not just leave it where it lay and we all had a very hard time trying to persuade it to get up. One of the cooks pulled it from the head and my brother from the tail, but it remained quite limp and flopped to the ground every time. At last it staggered to its feet but it was too weak and exhausted for me to ride so our cook put me on his horse, which was almost as weak and exhausted as mine was—too weak in fact to carry the two of us so our cook walked beside me leading my white horse.

Later in the day we came upon a sheltered place with good grass where our hungry horses could graze, so we camped and had lunch. We decided to rest the horses and have a little sleep ourselves—it would be safer and cooler to ride on during the night. I could not sleep at all but I lay down and tried to relax. The Khambas' news about the failure of the uprising in Lhasa and the stories we had been hearing of battles and arrests made me feel very worried and unhappy, I was very anxious about my parents and desperately wondered what might have happened to them.

As soon as the sun set we caught our horses and started off again. This time we had to ride all night, and as it grew darker I began to fall asleep as I rode along and it was not easy to stay on my horse. Once I fell off altogether but fortunately did not hurt myself. Our cook picked me up and helped me to remount, but I could not keep awake and after a time the cook thought it would be a good idea if I rode up in front of him. He lifted me on to his horse and we set off, leading my white horse beside us. This was a great improvement and I fell sound asleep almost at once. I had a very good sleep on horseback. I don't know how long we had been riding—when I woke up it was already morning. My white horse seemed very much better and when I rode it again it no longer collapsed.

We had breakfast by a river bank and the horses grazed happily whilst we took a long rest. We were in a completely isolated spot with no sign of habitation in any direction. We were entirely alone in a vast empty landscape and it all seemed deceptively peaceful.

Once again we rode through the night and before dawn came to a temporary Tibetan Barracks set up to check all the travellers passing through the area and to prepare a defence against possible Chinese attack. They demanded to know what arms we were carrying. Our group consisted of my uncle, my brother, my old abbot uncle, the Minister of Chumna (who had rushed to us at Tsela Dzong in the middle of the night without stopping to gather anything at all), his servant and our two cooks. Everyone, except me and the Chumna Minister, had their swords, and we also had two Injicadum (Lee Enfield rifles with bayonets) and two pistols. The officer who checked us prepared to confiscate these arms. He told us we were not allowed to take 'military weapons' beyond that point, although he did not say why.

My uncle refused to surrender the weapons and had a very long argument with him. In the end we were allowed to keep them.

In addition to our weapons everyone carried a ga-u, a small silver box containing either a round 'medicine' ball or a stamped picture of a god, according to taste. The most popular contents was a picture of Jigjig Maye, a sort of Tibetan St Christopher. The boxes had all been blessed by a High Lama and were believed to afford protection from bullets in battle.

Morning came very soon after we left the barracks and we decided to rest. Now we had a Tibetan garrison behind us we felt that if danger came from approaching Chinese we would know it was coming and for once we felt comparatively safe.

In this more secure state of mind we were able to have a very long rest and were feeling quite refreshed when we at last decided to ride on. We rode easily until we came to a small village at the foot of a mountain. High up the mountain a monastery, the Sangna Chuling, overlooked the village.

We had lunch at the monastery but hurried off immediately afterwards and rode on until well after the dark. The going was rather rough and became increasingly difficult as the track skirted the foot of the mountains. The horses stumbled and scrambled over rock-strewn ground, and we could hardly see the way. Finally it became so difficult we decided to rest for the remainder of the night.

Just after sunrise the next morning a group of people caught us up. They too had come from Sangna Chuling and brought us the news that not long after we had left the monastery the previous day the Chinese had arrived and burnt the monastery to the ground. Very few of the monks had escaped.

With this sharp and tragic reminder of our own danger all fears and sense of urgency returned and we saddled our horses quickly and rode on faster than ever.

For me all this was very confusing. No one told me what

was happening. I was puzzled to know why we should suddenly be running from the Chinese in such a fearful frame of mind. For most of my life they had occupied my country but their presence had not really made much difference to my way of life. I was too young to know of any political significance or undercurrents existing. So I just rode along with the others and did what they did, worrying about my parents and becoming increasingly homesick with every mile.

We were a much larger group now. The newcomers who had

The monastery is burning!

brought us the news of the burning of Sangna Chuling had joined up with us.

We hurried on through the night and after some time came upon a large group of Tibetans who were also escaping from the Chinese. They had made camp for the night and we decided to stop there and snatch a little sleep whilst the horses rested for they were still in very poor condition and we had ridden them quite hard during the past two nights.

When daylight came we could see that there were a great many Tibetans around us. It was not safe to travel in such a large group, we would be spotted and our escape route noted far too easily. We had heard that the Chinese were sending up spotter planes to locate groups of escaping Tibetans and then sending troops to bring them back. So far we had not seen or heard any planes but we did not want to risk detection. So before the other Tibetans had broken camp, we packed up and rode on our way.

It had not been my uncle's intention to make for India— he had intended to join His Holiness in the Pota-la in Lhasa —but now circumstances had forced us onto this route there was nothing to be done but to continue. With the Chinese so close and all round us, it would have been useless to do otherwise. We were not on the main route to India, but at this time the track was fairly easy to follow.

11

ALADDIN'S VALLEY

WE rode on through mountainous country, winding our way through the brown foothills of the Himalayas. There was no snow but we could see the white caps of the mountains ahead.

Quite suddenly, as we rounded the foot of a mountain, we came upon a valley. As we trotted down the mountain slope we could see that it was quite a small valley, very green and pleasant with a great deal of bamboo. To our complete astonishment, it was crowded with Tibetan tents, cattle and horses. As we drew closer we were puzzled to see that there did not appear to be any Tibetans moving about this seemingly packed camp.

When we reached the valley we found that it was indeed deserted. Lying everywhere on the ground and in the tents were every kind of valuable imaginable—an Aladdin's cave, or rather valley, of jewels, gold, thankas, silver household utensils, beautiful clothes, rugs and hundreds and hundreds of boxes containing silver coins; each box contained 1,000 silver coins about the size of a florin. These tongam (boxes of 1,000 coins) had been minted from Tibetan silver by the Chinese and issued as currency. Everyone's possessions lay abandoned and strewn over the valley and horses, mules and cattle grazed everywhere. There must have been over a million pounds worth of coin, valuables and animals left stranded and useless in that little valley.

When we had recovered from our amazement at the sight of all this abandoned property we looked at our surroundings more closely. As far as we could see the valley was a wedge of

A caravan travelling in Tibet

Bearers resting on a hillside above a glacier

(*above left*) Two of the Dalai Lama's bodyguards, all of whom are chosen for their height and physique. (*above right and below*) All that remains of two of the most beautiful and revered images in Tibet after the Chinese had stripped them of their gold leaf and jewels. The naked and battered heads swathed in the ceremonial scarves of pilgrims are now cherished by Tibetans in India

green thrust into the rocky mouth of the mountain and the only way out seemed to be by the way we had come. Hopefully our cook rode to the far end of the valley to see if it was safe, or even possible, to continue. On his return he reported that there was no way through, from the far point of the valley the route became immediately precipitous. We were in a complete *cul-de-sac*. No wonder the valley was overflowing with Tibetan possessions; it was obviously impossible to take them further. Nevertheless, as there were no people in the valley, it was equally obvious that there must be a way through of some sort, but it would mean leaving all our possessions behind. As it was we did not have a great deal with us. When we fled from Tsela Dzong we had taken comparatively few valuables with us—we were not to know then that we were to be completely penniless in a strange land.

We rode back to the end of the valley with the cook to see if we could find the route that everyone else must have taken. The sight of the towering, perpendicular cliff appalled us; not only would we obviously have to abandon all our possessions but we were doubtful whether it would be possible to take anything at all.

There was no other way through, somehow we would have to manage to climb that sheer rock face if we were to escape. It was growing late by now and there was nothing to be done but to get a good sleep and make an early start in the morning. We did not want to waste any time. We felt that the Chinese were still uncomfortably close on our heels.

That night we had no need to put up our own tent, we slept comfortably in one of the abandoned tents, which was crammed with the valuables and coin boxes the owner had left behind. I lay down and covered myself with a beautiful sheepskin quilt, but in spite of feeling quite exhausted I could not drop off to sleep. The prospect of the unknown hazards before me was mercifully vague, nothing in my experience having prepared me for the future, but the realization that the Chinese had suddenly become implacable enemies shook me completely. I remembered the jolly Chinese barber in Lhasa who had laughed

H

until he cried as he shaved the other half of my head to match
the side my brother had denuded in his 'home' haircut attempt;
I recalled the sentry at the entrance to the Iron Bridge who had
jokingly poked his gun in my stomach before allowing me to
run across to catch up the donkeyman. I had been a little afraid
of him, but not because he was Chinese but because I was afraid
he would stop me running away from school and I would not
get home to see my parents. My parents . . . that was it . . . that
was the real gnawing anxiety and unhappiness. If we were now
running from the Chinese in fear for our lives, what was happening to my parents? Must they run too? How could they
manage it, even if they felt they must? Our farm was high in
the mountains hundreds of difficult miles from the border. My
mother almost certainly would not attempt it and my father
would never consider leaving without her. The thought that I
would probably never see my parents again struck me like a
knife and I wished desperately that I had made a dash for home
when the truck had stopped at Medoh Kongka on our way to
Kongpo, and I saw the track leading towards my home stretched
so temptingly before me. How I wished I had not resisted the
temptation then. Now there was nothing to be done, the only
way to go was forward across the mountains to India.

My old abbot uncle grunted and tossed in his sleep and I
wondered how in the world he was going to scale that pre-
cipice in the morning. I was young and agile and I certainly
was not sure I would manage it, but uncle abbot was an old
man and getting frail. It had been several years since he had
retired from the Pota-la and he had been living a quite sheltered serene life with my uncle. Well, we would all have to
manage, or die in the attempt, because we could not stay in the
valley forever and we could not go back the way we had come.

At last I fell asleep and almost at once it was morning. We
had breakfast at first light and then made a pile of bare essen-
tials for our journey. We had no idea what lay before us or
how long it would take. In any case we must cut our loads to
the absolute minimum if we were to negotiate the perilous first
steps out of the valley with any prospect of safety. Priority

must go to food and cooking pots; warm bedding too we thought would be vital in the freezing mountain nights; we would need money, if not before, most certainly when we arrived wherever we were going, our paper money would be useless, the silver was too bulky and we had little else with us—the small amount of silver we managed to carry with us was exhausted long before we completed our journey.

Our sack of tsampa was carefully divided to give everyone a small package and we each took two bricks of tea. Next the smallest cooking pots and the teabowls were made into the smallest load possible and given to me, they were to be my responsibility. The others decided for themselves what else to take, my uncle felt it was important to take the rifle, we did not know what dangers we might encounter along the way. My brother wrapped his load in his quilt, when we saw it was not as bulky as we had thought it would be we all did the same with our quilts. Our cook, remembering the importance of meat in all Tibetan diets, decided to try and carry a small haunch he had cut from one of the many prepared carcasses abandoned in the valley, to supplement our small quantity of dried meat. Alas, he had not gone more than fifty paces along the precipitous ridge before he had to jettison the whole thing to save himself from falling.

From the moment we started from the valley we had a very difficult time. At first sight there did not appear to be even a toehold in the sheer rock face of the mountain, but on closer inspection we could see a narrow ledge about 3 feet above us and rising steeply off to the right round the shoulder of the mountain. Somehow I clambered up to the beginning of the ledge, only to discover that it was little more than a shelf barely a foot wide. At first it was extremely steep, almost vertical, and we hardly dared to draw our breath as we edged our way along sideways, our faces pressed to the rock face and our feet at 'a quarter to three'—the ledge was not quite as wide as the sole of my boot. Pressed hard against the rock, arms spread-eagled at our sides, we balanced, rather than climbed slowly upwards, clinging like flies to the mountain wall.

After what seemed to be hours but what can only have been about half an hour of this terrifying creeping along, the ledge broadened out a little like a window sill and after we had climbed about 300 feet it levelled out into a comparatively straight path up which we continued to climb until we came at last to a bushy pass where we could walk quite easily. Now we became enveloped in low cloud and the atmosphere was moist and foggy. Tall trees made everything dark and wet with their dripping leaves and the pass was choked with thick undergrowth, bamboo and tangled bushes. There was no path to speak of and we had to push our way through the dripping undergrowth yard by yard.

I felt very tired after the fearful climb, but whether this was from effort or fright I don't know—perhaps both. Anyway, I thought, if old uncle abbot can still keep going so can I, and I pushed on in the hope that my uncle would call a brief halt soon. The cloud continued to drift like spasmodic fog across our path and for minutes on end we stumbled blindly forward until the cloud lifted and we could push on more surely for the next few hundred yards in the clear but gloomy light filtering through the tall damp trees, until the next veil of cloud descended on us.

Finally we had crossed the pass and left the cloud behind. But now the undergrowth seemed determined not to let us through. Our cook offered to go in front of us and cut a path with his knife. It was a slow business but much less exhausting than fighting every bush to get past. Less exhausting that is for everyone except the cook!

Presently we saw a village tucked into a clearing in the bush. The people were Khalo (Upper Primitive people). Their huts were made of bamboo blades built on poles. They wore white Tibetan-style chubas and had bare feet. They spoke Kongpo dialect—they trade with Kongpo and are great pig keepers.

We did not want to stay the night there—we were still anxious to get on—so we passed by the village and continued to travel through thick wet bush. As we did not know the way to India my uncle had decided that the best thing to do was to follow the Tsangpo which he knew flowed into India as the Brahmaputra. But first of all, we had to find it!

We pushed on until it grew dark, when we found a cave in an outcrop of rock. It was starting to rain and by the time we had put our tsampa and tea in the cave to protect it from the rain, we found there was not room for all of us as well. No matter how we squeezed ourselves together, it was obviously impossible for everyone to sleep in the cave. The two cooks volunteered to sleep outside and went off to collect some big green leaves which made a temporary shelter for them. It was bitterly cold, the rain drummed through the leaves accompanied by a high wind which literally screamed through the cave. We managed to build a brief camp fire which gave us a little heat and light, but it soon petered out. The cave dripped with water and we were too cold, damp and cramped to sleep.

The next morning the ground was wet and soggy, but it was bright and the sky was very clear. We climbed higher up the mountain then turned to go straight along the side. Our cook was still leading and cutting his way through dense undergrowth. There was no proper path, we had to make our own track the best way we could. Sometimes we came to some bush too thick and tangled for us to get through at all, or our way was barred by huge rock faces covered with wet red moulds too steep and too slippery to climb. Then we had to retrace our steps along the track we had just hacked out and try to find a better way to go.

During this day we found the Syiom river that led down to the Brahmaputra and reached our first river crossing. It was a bridge consisting of two tree trunks. In many places the bark had broken away and the bare wood was smooth and slippery. Immediately behind this 'bridge' there was a cave, partly hidden by a huge roaring waterfall. Great plumes of spray constantly soaked the tree trunks as the furious waters hurled themselves down into the rushing white torrent far below. The roar of the falls reverberated into the cave behind and the noise was deafening.

We had to cross one at a time and our cook went first. He

reached the other side quite safely and looked round for some way to help the rest of us across. He chopped a long thin piece of bamboo, and after finding himself a secure foothold, he grasped the improvised pole firmly and passed the other end across the 'bridge' to each of us in turn, so that we had something to hold on to and could be guided across quite well. At times the spray from the falls fell across the 'bridge' like a thick wet blind and without the guiding pole any of us could have taken a fatal false step as we were shrouded in spray.

When it was my turn to cross, my heart was in my mouth. I had the kitchen utensils, and some tea, butter and salt on my back. They were always my duty to carry and at this moment they seemed more cumbersome than ever. The cook passed the guiding stick towards me, but it seemed very frail and its length made it wave about so that I had difficulty in grasping it. The thundering noise of the falls beside me, the thick clouds of spray and the white surge of the swift current far below me combined to make me feel dizzy. It was only about 8 metres across to the other side, but to me it looked like 100 perilous miles. At last I managed to grab the bamboo and cross, very slowly and, to my utter amazement, quite safely!

It was my brother's turn next and half-way across his right foot skidded on the bare slippery wood. We held our breath with horror but luckily he fell astride the logs as though riding a horse and bobbed himself along the rest of the way quite safely.

On the other side of the river we found a small path. We followed it thankful that for once we could progress comparatively freely without having to cut and thrust our way along yard by strenuous yard. We followed the path for some way and finally found ourselves in another Khalo village. There were several Tibetans there having a rest before continuing on their escape to India, but as it was only about noon we decided not to stop.

We were still in a wet, bushy mountainous region but now there was a track of sorts which we tried to follow. Sometimes it would fork in two, or even three directions, then we must decide which track to take. When we made a wrong choice sooner or later we realized our mistake and had to retrace our steps back to the fork and take the other track. All this took time, sometimes as much as half a day wasted in following the wrong track. The dense foliage of the tall trees obscured the sky almost completely for much of the time and it was impossible to gain a view so that we could get our bearings. For much of the time we lost the track entirely and just had to make our way by the clearest route we could find.

The path we had taken to the Khalo village in the morning had led us unexpectedly away from the river and it took us some time to work our way back towards it. More by good luck than good judgment we had taken the right direction and evening found us approaching the river again. It was dusk and time to look for a cave for the night. We worked our way down through the forest to the bed of the river. We clambered over and round rocks and boulders until we found a small cave. It was not a very good one; the river was just in front of it and made a great noise as it tumbled and threshed its way past the cave at a great speed. The cave was shallow and very cold but there did not seem to be any more thereabouts and it was too dark to walk much farther, so we decided to stay in this cave in spite of its obvious discomforts.

Once inside the cave the noise of the river was so concentrated that we had to shout at each other to make ourselves understood, in spite of the fact that the cave was so small that we were sitting shoulder to shoulder. In spite of the noise and the cold and the wet, I was too tired to be bothered by any of it and I slept very heavily.

We must all have been exhausted and slept much later than usual, the sun was quite high when we got up and had a leisurely breakfast.

It was my daily duty to take care of all the cooking utensils. This meant that I had to wash the pots and kettles and everyone's teabowls.

After breakfast this day I went off to wash the dishes in the river. There were many rocks of various shapes on the bank and I chose one which was large and flat and jutted out almost like a table overhanging the river. I climbed onto it and put the bowls on one side whilst I washed myself. Then I started to wash the bowls. The white water of the tumbling river surging noisily past my rock should have warned me of the speed and strength of the current, but I knew everyone had been almost ready to leave when I left the camp to wash and I was thinking more of trying to be quick than noticing the force of the river. I took one of the bowls and held it by the rim against the current in order to fill the bowl with water; before I could have a second thought the river had thrust the bowl out of my hand and it sailed and bobbed away into the distance. It would not have mattered if it had been my bowl, but, most unfortunately it belonged to my uncle! To me it was quite the worst thing that had happened to me since leaving Tsela Dzong and I could not even begin to think how to explain such a disaster when I went back to the cave. I washed the other bowls with great care as I tried to think of what to say about my uncle's lost bowl. In the end, I went back and said nothing about it to anyone. I packed everything in a long, cotton cloth and strapped it on my back and nobody noticed I was one bowl short.

As we set off, we again had to find our own way, there was no track. Almost at once we had to start climbing steeply, we kept the river by our side but there was no way through the vegetation along the banks and the edge of the river bed itself was too choked with huge wet boulders to be passable at this point. We followed the river as best we could, but throughout our journey we often had to make long tedious detours. Many times after a hard and gruelling 'sidetrack' we found ourselves back on the river bank, barely 100 yards from the spot we had had to leave it one or even two days previously.

We walked on for 3 or 4 miles, we could hear the river below us, but the jungle was too dense to enable us to see it. Suddenly we came up to an outcrop of tall rock which was too steep and slippery to climb and we descended to the river bed

again. Almost immediately the river disappeared into the foot
of a rocky mountain and there was no way for us to go either
through or up—there was nothing to be done but to retrace
our steps practically to where we had started after breakfast
and climb over the mountain we had just skirted. I was not
really much put out by the difficulties of travel on this morning, I was too pre-occupied with worry over the loss of my
uncle's bowl. I spent my time inventing various explanations
to account for its absence when we must eventually stop to
eat, but none of the excuses I had so far imagined seemed either
probable or possible and I almost welcomed this latest detour,
tired and hungry though I was. At least it postponed our meal
and the inevitable discovery of the missing bowl.

We backtracked for some way until we reached a point where
the jungle began to thin out and the ground began to rise very
steeply. For once it was not raining, but it was very wet under-
foot. We slipped and slithered as we tried to find footholds on
the now almost perpendicular face of the mountain. Fortunately
there were long roots growing in the sodden earth and hanging
down the mountain face like ropes, and by grasping a root we
could haul ourselves up from one precarious foothold to the
next. We carefully tested each root before trusting our weight
to it; some of the roots were so soft and sodden that they came
loose at the first tentative pull. Twice I nearly fell backwards
as a root came away in my hand but managed to save myself by
making a wild grab at the mountain and luckily finding strong
roots both times. Once my left foot slipped off a slim toehold
whilst I was groping with my right to find a forward pace and
I was suspended in space at the end of a root like a fish on a
line. It seemed hours before I could steady myself and fumble
for another foothold, but in reality I suppose it was hardly a
minute.

We climbed in this way for some time then the roots began
to thin out and finally ceased altogether. Now there were only
a few trees here and there, clinging precariously like us to the
mountain side. As always, our cook volunteered to be the 'trail
breaker'. He struggled forward to the nearest tree; it grew

almost at right angles to the mountain and he tested it carefully for strength before climbing onto it. He found a long, whippy branch which he cut to use as a pole, then, passing one end of this down to the next climber, he braced himself against the trunk of the tree and heaved and hauled us up towards him, one at a time. Then he would scratch and claw his way to the next tree and the whole process started again. We progressed in this way for some distance until the wet earth gradually gave way to rock and the trees disappeared. By now we were several thousand feet above the river but still the mountain reared its head high above us. Now we were above the treeline, we could see the top of an outcrop of rock which seemed to rise up from the very foot of the mountain. It must have been the top of the rock wall that had barred our passage that morning. It ran along the side of the mountain like a shelf, barely a foot wide and obviously the only way we could go.

As if he had not enough to carry, our cook added my pack to his own, so that I could negotiate this frightening ledge unhampered. But I had been carrying the load for so long that even after he had taken it my back still felt the weight and I seemed still to carry the pack.

We started across the ledge one by one, each one flattening his chest to the rock and edging along sideways, slowly and carefully inch by inch, hardly daring to breath for fear the expansion of his chest to suck in the air would topple him backwards off the narrow shelf. When my turn came I had to concentrate on not looking down. Accustomed though I was to mountains and heights, a glimpse of the river threading like cotton through the gorge thousands of feet below made me feel very giddy. Luckily it was not far across this ledge and we all crossed it safely.

Then we had to start the climb down towards the river again!

Climbing down was almost as difficult as climbing up! Again we found a few trees clinging to the rock face and the 'tree and stick' process had to be reversed. This time, our cook remained behind, his back to the mountain, his feet on the tree and a firm hold on a stick which we also grasped in turn. He braced himself against our weight as we slowly 'walked' our way down the stick, feeling for footholds as we went. When we reached the limit of the stick we had to cling like a limpet to whatever foothold we found until the cook had slithered to the next tree and it was our turn to take the stick again for the next descent.

Then the roots began again, and again each one must be tested before swinging our weight on to it and 'walking' down the cliff to the root's end, then finding and testing another.

At last we reached the foot of the mountain and found ourselves on a comparatively comfortable track alongside the river. We looked back and saw that the place we had tried to go through that morning was barely 200 yards away. The river had simply been momentarily swallowed by a slim but impassable pinnacle of rock, only to emerge almost at once in a thunder of surging white water. We looked at that short distance in complete dismay. To have spent such a day clambering up and down thousands of feet, only to find ourselves 200 yards farther along the road to freedom was indeed a disheartening experience. The only good thing, as far as I was concerned was that the way had been so difficult that I had had no more time to worry about uncle's bowl and we had not been able to find a suitable place to stop and make a meal. But now we had reached the river again and it was getting late. We were tired and hungry. It would not be long before my uncle thought of finding a cave and having a meal before we settled down for the night. Then my 'crime' would be discovered! Once more I began to concentrate on finding possible explanations for the absence of my uncle's bowl. I was not successful, I was too tired and too hungry to think of anything.

12

BAREFOOT BY THE RIVER

THE forest formed a dense green wall along the shore of the river as we walked along, picking our way through the rock-strewn scree and mud. At last we came to a small cave and my uncle announced that we would have a meal and spend the night in the cave. I greeted the promise of a meal with mixed feelings, although I was so hungry the problem of what to say to my uncle about his bowl was not solved and thoughts of what he would say when he found it had gone filled me with fear. It was a very serious matter—to every Tibetan his teabowl is his most valued possession, wherever he goes he takes his own teabowl—in our present circumstances it was a minor disaster. Apart from the fact that my uncle was a strict man demanding the highest standards of behaviour at all times, without his bowl he would have nothing in which to contain his meal. As preparations for the meal progressed and the moment approached to unpack the bowls I began to wish a cloud would descend and swallow me but I had no such luck and when at last the meal was ready of course it was discovered that my uncle's bowl was missing. My uncle asked me where I had put it. Where else could I have put it but in my pack, I thought wildly, as I sat very still and muttered "I don't know." I could not admit I had lost it in the river; now it was too late, I had said, "I don't know."

Someone suggested I had lost it on the way, perhaps I had slipped and it had fallen from my pack. "I didn't slip," I retorted indignantly, feeling more nervous and uncomfortable with every moment. There was an uneasy silence and then my uncle fortunately decided that he was not very sure himself whether he had passed the bowl over to me to wash or whether he had put it beside him on the ground and left it there. Everyone decided that this was what he must have done and I breathed a huge sigh of relief at being so easily released from trouble.

All Tibetan tea and tsampa bowls have deep lids to them and my brother gave the lid of his bowl to my uncle for his meal. Needless to say, when I went down to the river to wash the dishes I was very careful not to lose anything.

The cave we had found was comparatively warm and dry and we slept on until quite late the next morning. We were all now beginning to feel rather tired after these days of hard going and almost continuous damp cold. When it wasn't actually raining, which was seldom, the forest dripped with moisture and when the sun shone everything steamed like a Turkish bath.

Old uncle abbot kept up wonderfully well, never complaining or admitting to any tiredness or discomfort and rarely accepting a helping hand, although he must often have been exhausted. He was a great inspiration to me and often when I felt I could not put one foot in front of the other for even one more pace, I would glance at the grimly determined old man plodding silently along and I told myself if he could do it, well then I could and pushed on.

We walked or rather struggled along the shore. Every few yards we had to go either up or round huge rocks that were wet and slippery with spray from the raging river beside us and the eternally damp air. At last we saw a small clearing in the forest wall that still skirted the shore. We turned into it for a rest and saw there was plenty of dead wood lying about so decided to make a fire and have some lunch. Dead wood is better than cut wood for lighting fires. It has no sap and once the wet bark is peeled off the dry wood underneath burns up quickly and well.

We had our usual lunch of tsampa, tea and a little dried meat. We were having to be very careful with our food supplies. We had been able to carry so little away with us from the valley; the tsampa was already getting very low and the dried meat was almost finished.

After lunch, we continued on our way, following the river. Although the sun shone brilliantly and made a nice change from the rain, it was not too hot for walking but it was very difficult to find the way. Frequently our route along the shore was completely blocked by a barrier of impassable boulders and we had to turn off into the forest.

The cook was the pathfinder. He seemed to have a gift for it and since he was willing to lead us he became the accepted 'front runner'. He must have found it very exhausting. The bush we so often had to penetrate was taller than we were and very dense. Sometimes it became altogether impossible to go through it at all; then we had to turn back and try somewhere else.

Leeches and mosquitos were always with us. Such things are unknown in Tibet and at first they had been a great torment but now we accepted them as a part of our discomfort. Our clothes had become tattered by thorns as we floundered through the bush and ripped by the rocks we climbed.

My boots had worn away completely and I was now forced to go barefoot. At first my feet were very sore and often cut and bleeding from scrambling over sharp rocks, but eventually they hardened and were not so painful. This was just as well because as things turned out I did not have anything to wear on my feet for almost two years—when I was given a pair of wellingtons.

So we travelled on. When we could follow the river along its banks it was almost as difficult as fighting our way through the bush. The river itself was wide and its broad banks were liberally strewn with rocks and small sharp pebbles that cut my feet. Some of the rocks were gigantic and we had to go through, round or over them as best we could. It was a slow exhausting business but I preferred it to the bush. At least I could see some sky high above me and the river seemed cheerful as it rushed and rolled along beside me. But the rocks would become too steep to scale or the river banks would disappear altogether as the river angrily squeezed itself through a high, thin gorge; then we were sidetracked into the thick bush, struggling for hours round the side or over the top of a mountain and descending again only to find ourselves a few hundred yards further along our way.

We slept in caves and eked out our food with one frugal meal a day.

I don't know how many days we travelled in this way, I just followed along automatically, but at last, after a long day fighting our way round the shoulder of a mountain the undergrowth thinned out, and just before the sun set we came to a village. There were six or seven bamboo Khalo houses perched on stilts in a wide clearing on the hill side.

To our great delight, we found there were some other Tibetans already resting there and we decided to stay there for two or three days and have a rest ourselves.

The village headman came to greet us with friendly welcome. He was a trader and his second language was Kongpo dialect so we were able to communicate without trouble. He generously offered us the use of his hut, which was the largest in the village. The room he gave us was a good size but very dark; there was no window and the walls were black with wood smoke. The floor consisted of wooden planks full of holes through which I could see the ground several feet below.

The prospect of a really comfortable sleep in a dry room was very inviting after our long nights in cold damp caves and it was not long before we all settled down. Alas, we had a terrible night. We did not sleep a wink! We were invaded by seemingly millions of fleas and bedbugs. This was my first experience of such things, but I'm afraid it was by no means my last! We were awake all night scratching and I thought morning would never come. I much preferred sleeping in dripping caves to a room with bedbugs.

The tribe kept chickens and at long last the first cock cry signalled the approaching dawn. But this was only first light and still we lay scratching until the sun was high enough for our cook to see enough to make the breakfast. I was never more thankful for a sunrise!

After breakfast the owner of the hut insisted that we buy some corn from him. He told us it would be a long time before we came to another village. We bought about one kilogram, we could not carry more, and the Khalo accepted several of our precious silver coins in payment. Rather expensive corn! I did not see any corn growing, the khalos seemed to raise little else besides pigs, so perhaps corn was an expensive luxury to them.

Later in the morning we saw some other Tibetans arrive, planning to rest in the village for a day or two. One of them wanted to buy a whole pig for pork on their journey. He bargained with the Khalo for a moment or two, then they went off towards the pig pens and I wandered after them to watch the transaction. It was a shocking business. As soon as the Tibetan pointed out the particular pig he wanted, the Khalo hurled his spear right through the pig's stomach. I have since heard the expression 'to scream like a stuck pig' and I can vouch for the horror of the sound. The pig fell to the ground and lay there screaming horribly until the Khalo took his knife and cut its throat. Almost at once he started to skin it; this was too much for me, I returned to our hut followed by the Tibetan who had borrowed a room in a hut opposite ours. He had hardly reached his room before the Khalo brought the skinned carcase over to him. It was a horrible sight, pink and skinless, hanging up in the room. It seemed as though I could still hear the pig screaming.

Very early the next morning, after another sleepless night, we were roused from our beds by a Khalo who dashed into the hut crying that the Chinese were coming and were almost upon the village; then he ran out again on his way to warn all the other Tibetans. It was still very dark in the room. We gathered our things together as quickly as we could. As we hurried away the other Tibetans were also gathering up their belongings in a great rush. As I ran past the Tibetan pig buyer of yesterday I noticed that he had left it behind in the hut in his hurry. There were quite a number of Tibetans. We were all running as fast

(left) The Tibetan
frontier with Assam,
in winter

(right) A Kuki
village in Assam

(above left) Refugees newly arrived in Assam. *(above right)* Young monks, hungry and bewildered in India. *(right)* Rinchen Dakpa today

as we could to put as much distance as quickly as possible
between ourselves and the village, expecting the Chinese to be
upon us at any moment. There was no cover. For once we were
crossing a comparatively bare mountain, this made it easier to
travel, but also easier to be seen from a distance! We pounded
along, trying to get ahead of the other Tibetans. They were such
a large group; we realized it would be difficult to find caves
for all to sleep in when evening came.

But when it grew late and time to stop for the night, there
were no caves to be found. We were again in thick, tangled
jungle. There was nothing for it but to camp where we were, in
the forest. It was raining so heavily that we would have to make
some sort of shelter from the downpour if we were to rest at all.
But first we had to clear a space. The undergrowth was tangled
so densely about us that it was difficult at first to wield our
knives, but gradually we gained more elbow room and set to
work to gather some leafy tree branches to make a frame on
which to hang a yak-hair blanket as a makeshift tent. It seemed
to take hours, finding the branches, cutting them down,
dragging them along to our little clearing, arranging them so
that the blanket would form a shelter. It seemed endless but at
last everything was ready—and the rain stopped! It was very
annoying!

Next we had to find wood for our supper fire. Luckily we
used flint and stone to light our fires so at least we were spared
the irritation of trying to use damp matches. Everything we
possessed was completely sodden by the rain and the wet soggy
ground. We got the fire going quite well, only to discover that
in our haste from the village that morning. we had not only
left our expensive khalo corn behind but most of the little
remaining tsampa as well. Now we had only one small bag of
it between all of us, so instead of a bowl of tsampa each, our
cook put a little tsampa in one big pot of water and made a sort
of creamy soup. We lived on one bowl of this soup a day for
quite a long time—until the tsampa ran out.

In spite of the light supper and drenched surroundings, I slept
surprisingly well until I awoke with a start next morning to

I

hear my uncle shouting for help. He leapt out of his quilt in great alarm as we all hurried to him to see what was the matter. He had woken up to find a long yellow and black striped snake curled up asleep beside him. As we gingerly pulled the quilt aside the snake slid away into the undergrowth.

It was decided that it would be best to have our daily bowl of tsampa soup in the evenings, so after a breakfast consisting of a drink of hot water, we gathered up our things and set off through the bush in the direction of the river.

As we pushed on we were joined by most of the Tibetans who had fled from the village with us. They had also spent a wet uncomfortable night in the forest. I saw the man who had left his pig behind in the rush. He was very annoyed with himself for his forgetfulness!

The undergrowth now thinned a little; we still had to cut and hack our way through, but it did not clutch at us quite so closely. The morning mist lifted as the sun began to slant through the trees, piercing the green gloom with golden lances of light. Quite soon the mountain turned away from us and we were confronted with another bridge to cross.

This one was made of bha (wicker). It was about 50 feet long and very high above the river, which looked no more than a single thread of silk as it threaded its way through the gorge.

The bridge was a woven semi-circle of bha, waist high and very fragile looking. There was practically no wind which was just as well; although we crossed one at a time, from the very first step, the bridge started to sway from side to side like a swing. The sway increased with every step, until there was danger of swaying over the top in a full circle. After every few paces, whoever was crossing must stand quite still until the swinging subsided. The minute they started forward again the bridge swayed with increasing momentum until they halted again to avoid being tipped out into space. It took a very long time for each person to cross; we had to patiently wait our turn. I was not encouraged by watching the perilous crossings of the people ahead of me!

Finally my turn came. I waited until the bridge settled down from the last crossing, then stepped on to it very slowly and carefully. I found that the sides of it came right up to my shoulders, which made it difficult for me to get a good hold. The *bha* was thin and pliant and I grasped the sides with a forward grip to pull myself along. Perhaps I didn't know how to do it, or perhaps my forward pulling motion had a bad effect, but whatever the reason, the bridge began to sway violently almost at once. I stood stock still, not daring to breathe, forced to take a grip ahead of me, because of the height of the sides I found it difficult to hold on at all. At last the dizzy swinging subsided enough for me to take a few more tentative steps, but immediately the bridge took up the sway again finally swooping so violently that I lost my grip and was flung into the bottom of the bridge; I had not yet reached the middle where it sagged more protectively. Terrified, I lay in the bottom of the 'basket', swinging from side to side in a sickening arc, convinced that each sway would be my last and I would tip out headfirst to be hurled into the white river water thousands of feet below. I could not make myself move at all, I was completely paralyzed with fear. I lay there as motionless as a log. Probably my very stillness saved me; at any rate, the bridge gradually settled until it stopped, but still I could not bring myself to move.

No one dared to come to my assistance, the bridge was far too frail and lurching to support more than one person at a time. Everyone began shouting to me to get up and go on but each time I moved the bridge started to sway and I froze again. I could hear my uncle and brother shouting above the others, urging me to pull myself together and at long last I managed to get into a kneeling position and gingerly edge myself onto my feet. I took the longest time of all to cross, pausing after each step until the bridge was still, but at last I reached the other side, trembling with fear and willing hands helped me onto the track where I sat down to recover whilst I waited for my uncle and brother to come across.

Once up the slope on the other side the path was quite good. We walked along comparatively easily until we came to a small grass clearing where we thought it would be pleasant to rest and have a little to eat, we were all rather hungry. We had finished the tea some days ago and there was only a very little tsampa, but quite unexpectedly we found a little dried meat in the bottom of my uncle's pack. He had carried it from Tsela Dzong. In the clear dry air of Tibet dried meat will keep sweet for a very long time, but in passing through this wet steamy region it had become damp and smelt rotten. In Tibet we would have thrown it away in disgust but in our present situation it was as welcome and luxurious as a sirloin steak and we each devoured our share with relish !

We had just finished our snack when some of the other Tibetans arrived and started making preparations for their meal. We still did not want to travel as part of a large group, not only for fear of being seen by the Chinese, who looked for groups of refugees with 'spotter' aircraft, but also because of the difficulty of finding caves to sleep in. We packed up our things quickly and went on our way.

We left the clearing and followed the track, which was hardly more than a whisper through the trees, as it descended towards the river. The going was not too difficult. The undergrowth was less matted and tangled but the ground was like a wet sponge, slippery and dank with sodden leaf mould. We followed the track as it twisted down the mountain and ended in a small cove just above the river. There were several caves and we chose one that was big and dry and not too far from the river, which here glided quietly along between sloping banks of shale, peaceful and shimmering in the late afternoon sunlight. We were all tired and were soon asleep.

It was late the next morning when we woke up to find all the other caves had been occupied by other Tibetans who must have arrived during the night.

They were talking of resting in this place for a day or two. It was certainly quite a good place, for the first time we actually had a dry cave and it was roomy. We were all very exhausted and poor uncle abbot particularly was beginning to show the strains of the journey. My uncle decided that since we all needed a rest we could not do better than stay where we were. We could not delay too long, we still had no idea how much longer it would be before we reached India and our food supply was almost finished. In spite of these anxieties, the prospect of a brief rest was very welcome. The first thing I did was remove my filthy, torn chuba and have a refreshing swim in the river. Next I tried to beat as much of the mud and slush out of my chuba as possible but it was so torn and ragged that I was afraid of it falling to pieces altogether.

Later that day some newcomers arrived. They too had called at the Khalo village where the man had bought the pig.

They told us there had been no sign of Chinese at or near the village; but the Khalo had played the same trick on them, routing them out of the huts early in the morning with shouts that the Chinese were coming. They too had rushed away leaving most of their things behind, including food the Khalos had sold them.

When we told them we had had the same experience, we all realized how the Khalos had cheated us. Later I was to meet many other Tibetans on whom the Khalos had played the same trick.

I am sad to say that there are many people who are the richer for the Tibetan refugees passing by with goods and cattle.

13

A DEATH AMONG THE ROCKS

WE rested for three days, spending most of the time sleeping or lounging about, trying to muster our strength for the next stage of the journey. Newcomers trickled in to the 'camp', tattered and tired, all with adventures to tell and glad to find a comparatively comfortable, secure place to rest for a day or two.

Until now, it had been considered safer to travel in small groups, but the region ahead was thought to be Dhenglo (Lower Primitive People) country and rumour had it that they were not too friendly, given to robbing small groups or lone travellers. It was decided to proceed in larger groups for safety and several Tibetans joined up with us when we decided to be on our way.

It was a sparkling sunny morning when we set off, still following the river which now twisted and coiled itself so tightly through the winding gorge that our way was constantly punctuated by bridges, all of which were terrifying—but some were more terrifying than others!

We came to one which was nothing more than a thick rope of entwined vines flung nonchalantly across a chasm. The only possible way to cross was upside down, with legs and arms thrown over the rope, suspended like a monkey on a horizontal stick. Thank goodness it was decided that this bridge at least was too dangerous and another route must be found. Only a very few, reckless Tibetans decided to attempt this bridge; most of them, like us, preferred to go a longer way round.

The river would have to be crossed but we hoped to find a

more substantial bridge further on, We were again in densely
forested country, the only way to go was up and then round
the shoulder of the mountain. Our cook resumed his job of
pathfinder, there was no indication that anyone had ever been
on the mountain before. Although presumably someone had
thrown the vines across the chasm and used the 'bridge', there
was no track—nothing. We tried not to stray very far from our
only guide, the river, but as usual we could not always follow
it closely and often had to go up or round a mountain before
we could get back to it again.

We pushed and cut our way through the thick bush, climbing all the time. As we climbed higher the entangling undergrowth gradually thinned until at last the ground became
comparatively clear and we could climb almost easily through
the trees that still spiked the mountainside.

Almost as soon as we reached this more open ground the vast
silence trembled into a roar. After the first shocked moment we
realized it must be an approaching aircraft. We were soon in
no doubt—we could see it, glinting in the sunlight. It must be
a Chinese plane searching for Tibetans and their escape route!
Fortunately the mountain was still fairly liberally spread with
trees and bamboo. We could now see the plane quite easily but
thought it was probably not so easy for him to see us. All the
same we scattered quickly for shelter. The cook and I hid under
a big bamboo tree. The plane came right over our hiding place
flying very low. It circled round several times, evidently searching, before it flew off into the distance towards the north.

We waited until there was no longer any vestige of sound
before we ventured into the open again. Now all our sense of
urgency and anxiety returned. We had no idea how far we had
come in actual distance; perhaps after all we were still not far
from the Tibetan border and Chinese troops could be upon us
within hours. We remembered the Khalo village warning. Perhaps the Chinese were really only just behind us and had
requested the plane to be sent up to check on our position. We
could not be sure we had not been seen from the air, or for that
matter whether the plane was Chinese or Indian. We were

more inclined to think it was Chinese; it was known that they did send planes to search for escaping Tibetans. As soon as everyone had emerged from their hiding places, we gathered together and hurried on, carefully tracking our way through the trees, ready to take cover at the first hint of pursuit.

We travelled hard for three days, up, down, over or round mountains. Now and again we came to the river and followed the banks for a short distance, but sooner or later our way would be blocked by a rearing boulder or unscaleable cliff and we had to detour through thick forest. Since avoiding the 'vine-rope bridge' we had still not come upon an alternative and were trudging a very long way round; sooner or later we *must* cross the river, but until another bridge appeared we were travelling very much out of our way, looping round the mountains on the wrong side of the river.

At last, we came to another wicker bridge, not as long or high as the last one, but obviously much older, and apparently disused—the originally yellow *bha* had turned blue with age and rot. The natives would not bother to come so far down the river when they could use the vine bridge higher up. Clearly we were going to have to risk it. We were becoming more exhausted and hungry with every day that passed, and since we had seen that aircraft, fear of pursuit and capture was an ever-present spectre that urged us to hasten towards freedom.

We watched several of the Tibetans ahead of us cross the bridge in safety before we decided to try it ourselves. After my terrifying experience on the last *bha* bridge, I was very reluctant to try this one. By the time my turn came to cross, I felt almost too frightened to make the attempt, but my uncle and other Tibetans were behind and my brother had crossed ahead of me in safety. There was nothing to be done but to face it.

I had not taken two paces before the bridge started to sway violently. The gorge narrowed at this point and all the waters of the wide fast flowing river were crammed between the rocky cliffs. The compressed volume of the frothing current was immense as it boiled and spat round huge boulders just below me. I stood stock still, clinging to the frail sides of the bridge, and stared down at the angry water that rushed round the rocks in a foam of rage. The bridge seemed to swing higher and higher and I felt giddy and sick with fear. The river boomed and thundered as it squeezed itself through those confining cliffs and they flung the noise back at it in resounding echoes, which simply added to my fear. I stood there swaying crazily, hypnotized by the torrent beneath me and quite unable to move. Everyone was shouting at me, telling me to hold tightly to the rim of the bridge and not to look down. They all shouted something different, but the more they warned me of the dangers the more confused I became until I did not know what I was doing. When I looked at the floor of the bridge I could see it was full of holes where the wicker had rotted with age. People behind me shouted so insistently not to look down that at last I started gingerly forward, holding the yielding rim and trying to keep my gaze fixed straight ahead. Not looking where I was putting my feet, in such a situation, it did not surprise me that after only three paces, the whole of my right leg slipped through one of the many holes I had seen in the bottom of the bridge, which immediately began to sway more violently than ever.

I couldn't get my leg out of the hole, the bridge swung from side to side like a demented pendulum, the spray of the waves breaking round the rocks below soaked my leg with glacial water as it stuck through the bottom of the bridge and I could get no leverage or grip to release myself. When I tried to pull myself up by the rim, the soft sides of the wicker crumpled and cracked towards me and I was perilously near to being tipped out altogether. As I had stepped into the hole, my leg, stepping into space had unbalanced me so that I had fallen onto my left knee and I found it impossible to get out of that kneeling position no matter how I tried. The more I struggled, the more the bridge swayed and swooped through the air and the icy spray stabbed at my captured leg like a thousand needles. I was sick with terror and began to think I was trapped there forever.

At last my brother stepped carefully onto the bridge to come to my assistance. Ignoring everyone's shouts that it would not hold two people at once, he advanced slowly step by step towards me. He half pulled and half lifted me by the shoulders; the bridge shivered and clacked but it held and at last my leg came out of the hole. Numbed by the freezing water and bleeding with cuts from the sharp, broken wicker, it almost gave way as I stepped forward onto it but my brother gave me his hand and led me gradually across to safety.

Accident on the bridge

By this time it was getting late. For once it was not raining, but the sky was cloudy and dark with the threat of rain. We started to look for a cave as we went along but it was some time before we came across a group of caves, only to find they were all occupied by the Tibetans travelling in front of us.

We were now passing through the Denglo region and decided it was too late to travel on in safety in search of a vacant cave; it was wiser, if uncomfortable, to stay where we were and sleep in the open with Tibetans nearby. In this region we believed there was safety in numbers.

It was beginning to rain again so we looked about for some sort of shelter. We found a tree growing outwards from the base of a steep rock wall. It was quite big, and to make it more or less rainproof we flung a yak-hair blanket across it to make a roof and had quite a good shelter. This done, I went off to collect wood for a fire.

For supper, our cook boiled some water and we each took our now empty tsampa bags and slapped and shook them over the water to sprinkle the last remnants into the pot.

That was the end of the food, we had nothing more. It was now almost a month since we had fled from Tsela Dzong. We had no idea how much farther we had to go to reach the Indian border, nor how long it would be before we reached a village where we could perhaps buy some supplies.

Anyway, the 'soup' that night was quite nice and we enjoyed it more than we thought we would.

Next morning for breakfast we had boiled water. We had plenty of boiled water in the days to come and at least I was saved the chore of washing up!

After breakfast we started off again. Almost at once the route along the river bank became impassable and we had to start climbing. We had not gone far before the trail became one of the very worst we had yet encountered.

At first it was densely matted with almost impenetrable bush, head-high and lashed and entwined in a tangle of thick vines. Huge roots snarled over the sodden earth to trip us as we squelched through the semi-darkness of the dripping under-growth. But when we tripped we did not fall to the ground, the bush was too thick for that, we simply toppled forward into the tangled brush and skidded and slipped onto our feet again. To me the greatest nightmare were the revolting ubiquitous leeches, which in this part of the forest seemed to be more numerous than ever. My boots had worn away long ago, my clothes were in tatters and the leeches were delighted to find so much unprotected flesh!

The first few days after my boots fell to pieces, it had been very painful and uncomfortable in bare feet. Now they had hardened and I had grown used to it and didn't really notice; but climbing that mountain without shoes was most unpleasant.

We were climbing diagonally. The ground gradually became

less entangled but smooth and slimy so that I slipped very often
and fell to my knees. Presently we came to an almost perpendicular rock wall dappled with small plants thrusting out of the
many rifts in the face. They were firmly embedded in the rock
and we were able to cling to them for balance as we levered our
way cautiously along a meagre cleft across the rock. We were
very high and the rock was very steep. Looking down, the river
was no more than a slim steel blade carving its way through
the compressed green jungle below.

The cleft was so narrow and dangerous that it was impossible
to cross carrying a pack, in spite of the fact that our loads were
now very depleted. Everyone had to split their load into several
small bundles, and make two or three perilous trips across the
ledge until they had all on the other side. As always on the
very dangerous places, our cook helped me by going across first
and dropping his pack before returning for mine. I still carried
the cooking utensils and it took our cook two crossings to carry
them across.

Although traversing the rock face was dangerous, it did not
hold the terror of the bridges for me. The hazards and excitement of rock climbing are familiar to every Tibetan and a good
head for heights a natural inheritance, so, although I would
not voluntarily have crossed such a ledge at home in Tibet, I
felt there was an element of adventure about it and was not
paralysed with fright as I was when we crossed the bridges.

Once safely on the other side we stopped to watch some other
Tibetans, who had come up behind us, to see how they managed
the crossing. One or two of them did as we had done, bringing
their loads across in instalments. I noticed that one of the
approaching Tibetans was carrying a short sword strapped
across his stomach and a very small pack on his back. As he
was about to start across the ledge, some Tibetans still waiting
to cross behind him, advised him to take his sword from his
waist and hang it horizontally down his back. He told them
that he did not think it was necessary, but I suspect that this
advice had put an idea of the danger into his head and made
him a little nervous. At any rate, as he started going across,

with his face pressed to the rock face and holding on to the plants as we had done, his sword must have touched the rock and pushed him backwards. He cried out only once as he fell outwards in a backward dive and plunged headfirst onto the rocks of the river bank thousands of feet below. We looked down and could just discern his body, motionless and crumpled and quite dead.

This misadventure naturally made the Tibetans still waiting to cross fearful of the attempt. The women in particular were very afraid. Some of them had very small children with them and two of them were carrying babies on their backs; they wanted to find another route even if it took a week or more. But their men were firm and told them they must not think of the accident and being afraid; they must concentrate on the way they were going. I think they were all probably without food, as we were, or at least getting very short, and could not afford to embark on a long, uncertain detour.

After seeing the young man fall to his death we did not care to watch any more crossings. We set off again along the side of the mountain. We were now quite near the crest and the going was not as rocky and narrow as it had been; but it was slippery, which was just as dangerous. One slip and we would hurtle thousands of feet down to the rocks below with nothing to break our fall. We stepped very, very slowly, trying to set our feet into small hollows of rock and wet soil so that we could brace ourselves against sliding as we began to descend the mountain again.

When at last we had slithered to the foot of the mountain in safety we refreshed ourselves with a bowl of boiled water before setting off again.

The forest was now not quite so dense and our cook spotted some plants with large green leaves which we recognized from Tibet as edible. We were overjoyed by his discovery but then came disagreement. Some said walk on we would find more later, others said pick them now while we saw them, there might not be more later. Personally I was so hungry that I could not understand how there could be any argument, I wanted not only to pick them but eat them at once. In the end we did pick them but we did not eat them until the evening, when we had a sort of boiled green-leaf soup which would have tasted better if we had had some salt to add to it—even so, it was not unpleasant and quite filling. Afterwards I had to wash up once more! As it turned out, there were plenty of these leaves in this part of the forest and we lived on green-leaf 'soup' without salt for the next four or five days.

At last we reached another village, but to our surprise and some disappointment we still seemed to be in the Khalo Region, which meant that we had not travelled as far in actual distance towards the safety of the border as we had hoped in spite of the fact that we had been battling along for nearly three weeks. What with having to climb up, down and round mountains and carve a track through almost impenetrable jungle, it sometimes took three days of trekking to follow 3 miles of river.

The Khalos were friendly enough although they dressed rather differently from those of the previous villages. Instead of white chubas, they wore nothing but a hollow buffalo horn strung on a thong round their hips which in that steamy humid atmosphere was more than adequate for warmth in the daytime but I should have thought it rather chilly in the cold damp of the nights!

We decided to stay for two days in this village for a rest. The first thing we did was buy something to eat. The Khalos had only corn, pork and salt, but after our meagre soup and water diet of the past days such food was luxury. The Khalos let us have one small piece of pork, a little salt and one small bag of corn in exchange for my brother's quilt, and for supper we had a feast of boiled corn soup with pork and salt.

The huts were exactly the same as in the last village. Plaited bamboo-blade walls, a dried long-grass roof with a platform floor balanced on pillars. The pillars had long bamboo fencing round the foot to make an enclosure for the pigs beneath the hut. Steps up to the hut were formed by a 'ladder' made from an old tree trunk chopped roughly into steps which we found very slippery and difficult to negotiate.

We asked if we could borrow a room for a couple of days and the village Headman agreed to lend us his 'hall', a large unfurnished room almost pitch dark inside, the only light creeping dimly up through the floor boards, which were about one inch apart. Looking down through the cracks in the boards I could see the pigs . . . and smell them! They were very overcrowded and noisy, grunting and squealing in argument over scraps of food.

The floor of the hut was filthy, I don't think it had ever been swept. The boards were coated with black grime and smoke and littered with bones, stones, sticks, pigs hair and scattered ashes of countless fires. We had to sweep the room thoroughly before we could think of using it; but it was impossible to make it really clean, the filth was too ingrained. I looked at the unsavoury surroundings and thought longingly of the beautiful rooms at home with the polished furniture mirrored in the gloss of the spotless floors. I wondered how anyone could bear to live in such a disgusting room, even in the daylight the walls were alive with bedbugs and we were not surprised to find that sleep was almost impossible at night when fleas and bedbugs descended on us in their hundreds and enjoyed a rare feast!

In spite of these discomforts we rested in the village for two days, enjoying the temporary respite from endless trail breaking and climbing and relishing hot corn soup and pork.

When we were preparing to continue our journey, our host offered to come with us to help with the loads and show us the way which he said would be very dangerous, with many bridges difficult to cross. He was willing to guide us for one week and in exchange for his help, he said, he would like one of our guns, the Injicadum (Lee Enfield). We were reluctant to agree to this. Our precious gun seemed to be rather more than a fair exchange for what after all was a routine trip for our host, to whom the trail and bridges were a regular trading route; we remembered through what odds we had clung to our rifle, the long argument with the officer at the Tibetan guard post, teetering over precipitous rocks and ledges, swaying and slithering across bridges but always clinging to the rifle as a defence, certainly a forlorn one, but at least a small resistance to possible Chinese attack. But on the other hand we thought it was undoubtedly true that the way ahead was difficult and dangerous, it would be much safer and quicker with expert guidance. In the end, we accepted his offer and then found we had to give him the gun before he would consent to leave with us because he wanted it to be left behind in his hut.

He escorted us himself and two of his sons carried our loads. We set out before sunrise and noticed that several other Tibetans were coming with us accompanied by villagers who carried their loads for them. It was marvellous to be unhampered by a pack, but after our experience of the 'Chinese are coming' trick in the previous village we did not feel we could trust the natives, we were afraid they might well make off with our few remaining possessions. The trail was difficult for us and dangerous but the natives travelled very fast and were expert at negotiating the precipitous climbs and precarious toeholds that constantly confronted us. It was difficult to keep up with them and several times we had to call to them to slow down. When we came to a particularly hazardous climb they went ahead very quickly, bounding from toehold to toehold with the agility of mountain goats, deposited our loads at the top of the cliff then returned to our assistance. Grasping our wrists in a vice-like grip and bracing themselves in the footholds they seemed to find by instinct, they pulled us upwards yard by yard until at last we reached the top only to be faced with an almost perpendicular descent down a rock-lined ravine or, worse still, a finger-wide ledge crossing a cleft in the rocks or another hair-raising bridge across a raging torrent of white water hundreds of feet below.

In spite of being free from my load for once, I had carried it for so long that I could still feel the weight of it and occasionally rubbed my back to convince myself that it was not still there. I was very hampered by leeches continually sticking to my bare feet and legs, which were already covered with purple marks from many previous bites and my tattered chuba was constantly saturated by the interminable rain which now beset us; being made of wool it absorbed rain like a sponge and became very heavy.

The first evening we found ourselves a cave as usual, but our guides didn't bother about shelter, they just sat under a tree. When we had prepared our supper from the frugal supplies of corn and pork we had brought with us from the village we discovered that we were expected to feed our guides as well, which they had neglected to mention when we started out. They had large appetites too! Fortunately they were expert fishermen and caught and prepared some river fish to supplement their share of the supper. Although the rivers and lakes in Tibet teem with fish, we never eat them or fish for sport. It is against our religion to take life in any form; at home the meat, that is essential in Tibetan diet, was always butchered by a special man called in for the job which was handed down from father to son. It never occurred to us to 'kill for the pot' during our escape, not even when we were entirely without food of any kind.

The following day we had a very difficult time, when we were not floundering through a sea of vegetation we were staggering and skidding up and down mountains that were often so steep that the only way to go upwards was on all fours and downwards almost flat on our backs.

The trail twisted through a tunnel of tangled vines and bamboo which towered over my head in a canopy so entwined that the path was wreathed in an eerie gloom, making it impossible to tell dawn from dusk except by weariness. We seemed to be engulfed in a somnolent immensity of silence broken only by the monotonously dripping leaves. We squelched along in single file through the dank sodden leaf mould until without warning we emerged on the crest of a ravine and found ourselves facing another bridge. It was not a very long one but it looked very perilous. The river below was black with depth and fought its way with compressed strength through a steep narrow gorge. The bridge consisted of two parallel vine ropes with boards laid across them at intervals. Marks had been

K

made in the centre of each board to show people where to step.

Our guide went across first with speed and nonchalance. He knew we would not be able to do this and told us not to follow him—we had no desire to do so! He put the loads down on the far side and returned to help us across. He held out his hand and prepared to lead us one by one. We were told to be sure to place our feet on the centre mark of each board and warned that if we stepped to the side on any of them, it would tip up and throw us into the surging river below!

I had no difficulty in crossing because he carried me over on his back!

14

TRAINS AND BOATS AND PLANES

WE trekked along in single file behind our guides as they pushed their way through the dense vegetation of the mountainside, struggling up steep ridges and down into deep ravines between them, then up again to crest another ridge; even without my load to carry I found it exhausting work and as we reached the top of each ridge I hoped fervently that it would be the last, but there was always another one ahead; they rolled before us under their thick canopy of jungle like an endlessly undulating dark-green ocean.

At last we stopped beside a sizeable hollow in the hillside where a heavy tree had fallen during the monsoon, torn by its roots out of the spongy ground. It made quite a good shelter and we decided to camp for the night. In the gloom of the forest the sunlight did not penetrate very strongly to disturb us and it was quite late when we woke the next morning, to an ominous stillness. There was no sign of the Khalos; they had abandoned us during the night and gone back to their village, after guiding us for only two of the promised seven days! We decided it would be useless to return to their village and start again; the only thing to be done was to shoulder our loads, which they had fortunately left behind, and try to find the way ourselves as best we could. Although we were still following the river, we were high on the side of the trackless hillside. It was not very steep but matted with bamboo thickets, dripping fern trees and dense tangles of undergrowth which towered well over our heads. The silence yawned about us like a somnolent giant, even the "chack chack" of our cook's knife as he hacked at the bamboo barring our path was lost in the depths of the bush that flanked our sides.

We struggled on for what seemed to me like a lifetime, cutting and tearing a trail across gully and ridge after gully and ridge, on and on through the oozing gloom. It became almost mechanical to me to slip, slide, heave and push my way yard by yard along the trail. I hardly noticed the leeches feasting on my bare legs nor the fruit flies and mosquitoes that swarmed to feed on the drying blood of recently vacated leech bites.

At last the vegetation began to thin out and we came to a rock-lined ravine across which we could see a village set quite high on the side of the bare mountain that faced us. We clambered across the rocks and approached the village with some caution until, to our astonishment, a woman, obviously a Tibetan, came towards us and spoke in Tibetan, As she was speaking my old uncle abbot suddenly recognized her as a girl who many years before had left Tibet with her mother to make a pilgrimage to India. On their way home to Tibet she had met and married a Khalo and settled down in this village.

We stayed the night in her house and the following morning my old uncle announced that he was going to stay on for a while to recover his strength. He was very old, very tired and very sick. It had amazed and often encouraged me along the way to notice how bravely he had struggled this far but I could see he was very nearly at the end of his strength. As we left him I tried to smile when I said good-bye, but I felt very sad thinking I would never see him again.

After another long and difficult day, we stopped for the night under a tree which grew outwards from a wall of rock. There were many banana trees. They were not in fruit, but we gathered some of the leaves to supplement the few that drooped on the tree and made a roof to our shelter. After a supper of corn and pork soup I lay down on the ground, soft with sodden yellow leaves, and fell asleep immediately.

The next morning, when I opened my eyes, I was terrified to see a dark-red growth, about the size of a man's thumb, sticking out of my chest. After the first paralysed moment of horror I pressed it gingerly and found it was viscuous and pliant like a balloon. I felt quite revolted and sick and very afraid. It seemed to me that I must somehow have got a hole in my chest through which some sort of gland was coming out. Half sobbing with fear and revulsion I ran to my brother who was still sleeping and shook him vigorously, begging him to wake up and look at the disgusting 'growth' on my chest. He looked at me sleepily and mumbled that I was not to disturb him, but the growth seemed to be getting bigger every moment and I was shouting now as I continued to shake him in increasing alarm until at last he woke up and inspected my growth with attention. As he scrutinized it he also concluded it was a large gland protruding from my chest. This agreement with my own 'diagnosis' terrified me even more and in great fear I rushed in panic to our cook. He very sensibly realized it was a leech as soon as he saw it. He covered it with snuff and it immediately fell to the ground. Then he stepped on it, pressing it with his toe until it burst, spreading red blood everywhere.

For me this still remains one of the most revolting and frightening experiences of the whole journey.

By now, the sun was beginning to leap up above the mountains and the sky was as blue as a turquoise. We had finished our pork and corn for supper the night before, so after a breakfast of hot boiled water, we shouldered our loads and with fresh morning breath started off on the trail again.

We saw no sign of habitation all day, the going was as hard as ever and I began to believe that there was no one in the whole world but us and no other world but these inhospitable tortuous mountains.

I followed along quite automatically until suddenly the whole mountain reverberated with thunder. I had hardly noticed the darkening sky and rising wind; the sudden explosion of sound made me jump as though someone had clapped my head between cymbals. The occasional scrubby trees that clung to the almost perpendicular side of the mountain trembled and bowed in the whip of the wind, lightning split the sky and seemed to strike the ground almost at our feet. Without one warning drop, rain deluged upon us and we were instantly drenched to the skin. There was no shelter of any kind to be seen; there was nothing to be done but proceed. We slipped and slithered through the rivers of muddy rain washing down the mountain side and I began to be afraid that I too would be washed into the river as it barged through the gorge we were skirting. With every step I tried to cling to the slipping mud with my bare toes until my feet ached with the effort and the cold rain. Often I flopped forward onto my knees, crawling along on all fours until I gained enough purchase in the sliding mud to stand upright again. The rain lashed into my face with such force I could hardly see; it formed a saturating, blinding glass curtain.

The storm left us as quickly as it had come, leaving the air grey and humid. Our ragged clothes dripped uncomfortably as we squelched along. It was getting dark when we eventually reached a village, where we found other Tibetans, who gave us the welcome news that we were at last not far from the Indian border and an army barracks. There, they had heard, supplies of food and clothing were given to all Tibetan refugees when they arrived. We were overjoyed by this news. It had taken us almost a month to complete a journey that the natives of the region took in their stride in a brisk ten days. But then they knew the way, they traded regularly with India and Tibet, and also, as far as I was concerned they were able to negotiate those terrible bridges quite fearlessly. I suppose because they had built them—if throwing a rope of vines across a chasm can be called building a bridge!

We left very early next morning, after a breakfast of boiled water, cheerfully looking forward to reaching the Indian barracks very soon.

Some of the other Tibetans joined us, and for the first time for many days we had bright smiles on our faces as we walked along, comparing adventures and telling each other about the difficulties we had encountered. Then they began to speak of people left behind in Tibet, wondering what would become of them. As we walked on and on I remembered my parents and the farm. Even in the midst of my anxiety for them I felt a surge of pleasure at the recollection of my truant visit. I was glad I had run away home from Norbulingka; I was even glad I had broken my arm, it had at least given me several months of additional happy memories of home—it was beginning to look as though this was all I would ever have. It already seemed to me unlikely that I would ever see my parents again and, in spite of the prospect of food and shelter, my heart was heavy and my thoughts despondent.

Enclosed in my remembrances of home, I hardly noticed the trail that took us down a steep ravine to the banks of the Gong-gnachulin. As the big red sun sank down behind the mountain, we found a cave and after a supper of boiled water we were soon asleep.

The following morning we went on until we had climbed to the crest of another mountain. Once at the top we could see the Indian barracks quite clearly, surrounded by many houses, apparently on the other side of the mountain. Almost light-headed with relief and delight, we all sat down to rest and stare at the glorious view of houses that spelt food and refuge for us. They seemed to be less than half a mile away, across a thick green tapestry of treetops. We all started speculating on the distance and how long it would take us to get there. Some said we would arrive early the following day; others, more pessimistic, said a week.

In the event, it took three days and they were the three longest days of the entire trek. We slithered and stumbled down deep ravines, clambered over huge wet rocks that littered and sometimes blocked the river bank, climbed laboriously up slopes of shifting scree when every step seemed to threaten an avalanche of shingle so sharp that it cut my feet, hardened though they had become since my boots had worn away. Once, after toiling almost to the peak of a steep cliff we were confronted by a vertical ridge of rock that was obviously impassable and we had to retrace our footsteps almost to the bed of the river again. This *impasse* delayed us almost a day and we decided to rest by the river for the night; the sun was setting and we were too tired to look for another way to go. It was discouraging that the barracks, which had looked so close, did not seem to get any nearer, no matter how far we laboured. Often after trailing up and down and round a mountain we arrived back at the river barely 100 yards away from the place we had left it several hours before. At long last, on the third day, we really knew that we were climbing up the mountain of the barracks. Our hearts were light as we climbed on and on. Some said they could smell the delicious food waiting for us, several people shouted gaily that it was the spicy aroma of mo-mo, a very popular Tibetan dish. It all seemed very exciting. I was hungry too; we had left without our usual breakfast of boiled water in our impatience to reach the barracks. Most of us had had no food for over a week. Although we had passed through a banana forest and were very hungry, no one had eaten the fruit; the younger Tibetans had tried but the older ones had told them not to. No one remembered the very old Kongpo poem that says: "When you are hungry go to the banana forest and eat the fruit; when you are cold, cover yourselves with banana leaves!" Or, if they did remember it, they did not associate the bananas surrounding them with the fruit of the poem. Not until we all reached Missamari, in Assam, where bananas were on sale in the bazaar, did we identify the fruit of the forest.

Our progress up this last mountain seemed interminably slow, but eventually, a little after noon, we arrived at long last at the barracks.

There were many other Tibetans already there. They greeted us warmly then asked us anxiously for news of relatives and friends left behind in Tibet. They scanned the faces of the newcomers hoping to welcome a loved one or a friend, but there were none amongst us.

Alas, the delicious aromas of food that had urged us so cheerfully up the final climb, were only imagination. It was not until we had given our names to the officer in charge that we were issued with our food supplies. We were then given rice, dahl, tea, sugar, salt and aluminium cooking pots. They had no clothes to give us so we stayed in our rags, but the Indians were very kind and did what they could to make us comfortable.

Their barracks was a long, low mud building painted white, with a big parade ground in front where I went to watch the soldiers doing P.T. every morning. I found their gymnastics very interesting. It is a favourite recreation in Tibet to build up our physical strength, especially for wrestling, a very popular pastime.

The village houses were made of bamboo and for the week we were in this camp we stayed with the village headman. At the end of the week we were feeling more rested and ready to move on; but before we left the Indian officer in charge told us we must hand over our guns and any other weapons, such as swords or knives. We were very sorry about this, we had been tempted many times to discard them along the trail but had always resisted the temptation because they gave us a small feeling of security. The officer, however, was adamant, no weapons of any kind were allowed; so we reluctantly parted with them all. Parting with their swords was especially difficult for the men who had carried them so far—to a Tibetan his sword is a part of his life and a personal history. They are often very beautiful, with engraving on the finely tempered blades and the hilt and leather scabbard embellished with gold or silver and precious stones. They have usually been handed down from generation to generation and some of them are literally several hundred years old. But we had already realized that sentiment for possessions has no place in the life of a refugee; the swords were handed over with the guns.

The onward trail from the barracks was comparatively easy. We followed well-beaten paths but they were often very wet and muddy. The lowering rain clouds, which sometimes swirled about us like fog made everything damp and humid. Occasionally the sun would break through, heating the forest about us until it steamed like a giant cooking pot. After several days of walking all day along these paths, sleeping in caves at night, we arrived at another Indian barracks where there was also

an airport. Here too there were many Tibetan refugees who
told us the name of this place was Daporijong.

The soldiers seemed to keep a constant supply of hot tea
ready for the refugees arriving daily at the camp and we joined
the queue for big mugs of tea.

Then we were told to go at once to the headquarters office to
register. Here the officer told my uncle that he must go to
Assam as soon as possible because His Holiness the Dalai Lama
was in need of Tibetan officials to organize the thousands of
refugees now streaming into India. The Indian officer told us
we were to leave by the first plane. I was very excited to hear
this. I had seen aeroplanes in the sky of course, but I had never
seen one land or take off. I hardly knew how to wait until the
time came for me actually to get inside one and fly!

The plane arrived three days later. We climbed in with room
to spare so were joined by some other Tibetans. As the plane's
engines roared into life and we started moving faster and faster
along the ground most of the Tibetans were saying their prayers
loudly and rapidly. This made me nervous too, but I had settled
myself by a window, and concentrated on watching the plane
lift up so that the ground fell away until we climbed above the
mountains, leaving them far below. I could just see the Syiom
river running down between the mountains like a long silver
snake. Presently it joined the Brahmaputra, which lay across our
route in a broad cable, and the tributary, our friend and guide
to freedom, was swallowed up in the broader waters.

Once I forgot to be nervous, I thoroughly enjoyed every
moment of the flight—until we started to come down and my
stomach started to lift into my throat. This gave me a slight
headache, but I still concentrated on looking down on the town
where we were going to land. I could see houses and all sorts
of vehicles moving beneath us, soon I could see people in the
streets. Everything seemed to be gliding past me in slow
motion. Then the ground came up to meet us and we had
landed at Sadiya airport.

The sun was blazing, the air trembled with the heat which
struck me like a blast of flame as I got out of the aircraft. As

I stepped on to the ground, the paving burned my bare feet so fiercely I did not know how to walk the short distance to the truck that was waiting to take us. Worse was to come when we got in to the truck. I don't know how long it had been parked in the sun, but its naked iron floor and metal sides were red hot to the touch. It was like an open oven. We all hopped about from foot to foot in a painful 'fire dance', trying not to over-balance and come in contact with anything; whatever we touched burnt us.

We must have looked very unusual, with our gaunt tired faces and tattered clothes, hopping about like dancing puppets in the back of that truck. No wonder the people of Sadiya stopped to stare in amazement. Fortunately the journey only lasted about a quarter of an hour, then we came to an empty house where we were to stay the night.

We were given some food and told we must continue our journey by either train or bus. I hoped it would be by train. I had never seen one but I remembered my mother used to tell me that a train was a combination of many houses driving on an iron road. She had never seen one either, this was what she had heard, and in my imagination I always thought of this train of houses being driven along on a vast flat area of thick iron sheeting. Thinking of this iron sheeting, the very hot airport and the burning hot truck, I decided that people travelling by train must be terribly hot.

However, next morning it was decided that we should go by bus to catch a boat across the Brahmaputra to Tezpur. One of the Indians looking after us took us to the bus station and put us in the bus, which was crowded with Indian passengers. I sat beside an Indian with a very dark face, a yellow turban and orange teeth. I was quite struck by the colour of his teeth; Tibetans generally have very white, strong teeth. Later on, of course, I saw many Indians with orange teeth from chewing betel nut.

The bus journey was a long one. I got very hot and cramped —but I saw my first real train! The bus had to pull up to let it go by and as I watched carriage after carriage roll past, I thought my mother was not really so far out, it did look rather like a series of long narrow houses on wheels. But I had not pictured the rails correctly at all, they were nothing like the wide iron road of my imagining.

When the bus arrived at the harbour we were all asked to go into the ship that was waiting. I was much more surprised to see the ship than I had been by my first close view of an aeroplane. I had certainly heard people talking about there being ships in India, but I had no idea what they meant and had never been able to imagine what they could be like. The ship we were on seemed very big. I stood on the deck watching all kinds of goods, passengers, cars, lorries and even trains coming aboard. I was completely astonished, I could not believe that a ship could be loaded with so much without sinking to the bottom of the river. But I saw other ships sailing back and forth, they seemed to be floating very nicely so I assumed that we would cross quite safely too.

As I stood by the rails the dark Indian who had sat beside me in the bus came and stood next to me. We watched the activity on the dock below in silence then he gave me a small coin and strolled away.

It was a very slim copper coin. When I showed it to my uncle he gave me permission to go to the shop on the deck below and spend it. When the shopkeeper asked me what I wanted, I pointed to some biscuits in a glass jar. He shook his head indicating clearly that the small coin was not enough for a biscuit and gave me five ground nuts in exchange for it. I went back to my uncle to offer him some, but he did not want any. I ate them all myself—they were very quickly finished!

Once the ship was loaded we were soon across the river to Tezpur, there we found a jeep waiting to take us to Missamari, a very big Tibetan refugee transit camp. The drive lasted about two hours. It was very dark when we arrived at the camp but in spite of this many Tibetans crowded round our vehicle— many of them were calling out names to us—hoping that a long lost relative or friend might be a member of our small party. We in our turn also tried to scan the faces of the surrounding crowd, hoping even in the darkness to recognize a friend.

We were led to one of the bamboo houses. There were over 100 of these shelters already put up in rows and many more were being built to accommodate the hundreds of refugees crowding into the camp.

The huts were long, narrow buildings with narrow bamboo platforms, raised about 2 feet from the earth floor and built round the walls like a shelf to make one long continuous bed, which was shared by as many Tibetans as could squash along it together. The camp was already overcrowded and new arrivals squeezed in almost daily. Running the length of the huts, between the sleeping shelves, was a 3-foot passageway.

Each hut had two kerosene lamps, one at each end. They gave very little light and the centre of the huts was in complete darkness.

Even if the huts had only contained the fifty people they were intended to accommodate, it would have been a tight squeeze. As it was, in every hut there was more than double that number at times. There were two small kitchens, one at either end of each hut, which was shared by the occupants. With twenty-five people trying to share one small kitchen, it was not easy to make food. Fortunately, most Tibetans are by nature helpful and co-operative towards each other. They had soon arranged to get one large cooking pot from the Indians, pooled their rations and each family took a turn at cooking a meal for everyone.

As we entered the hut and I saw the accommodation I was relieved to hear we were only to stay there one night whilst arrangements were made to accommodate my uncle more comfortably.

The crowd of Tibetans followed us into the hut, eager for the latest news of Tibet. I was very tired and longing to lie down to sleep. We did not get any bedding, so had to make do with our own, such as it was! It was not until the crowds began to dwindle away at long last that I had a chance to find a space to sleep. I put my one thin blanket underneath me as some protection from the roughness of the bamboo bed! It was very bumpy! The canes had been split in half, then roughly crushed with a knife in an attempt to flatten them a little, but the result was a series of sharp ridges and lumps which made it difficult to sleep, worn out though I was. There was no room to lie down properly, I was half sitting with my head and shoulders propped rather awkwardly against the end wall.

It was very hot and the air whined with hundreds of mosquitoes. I could hear my fellow Tibetans flapping cloths and blowing at them in useless attempts to keep them away. During this long restless night, I began to long for the damp chill of the caves we had slept in so often in the clear air of the mountains. They were certainly more comfortable than this stifling insect-ridden hut.

Completely sleepless and disturbed by the incessant stridency of the mosquitoes, the heat, the suffocating lack of air and the rustling of my room mates, my mind began to wander anxiously over the prospect of what was to become of me in the future and, as always, what had become of the family I had left behind. Altogether I spent a wretched night, almost the most miserable since our escape had begun. I was discouraged by the drab reality of our apparent journey's end; suddenly the heat and the insects and the squalor of it all, the hundreds of other homeless, ragged anxious Tibetans around me brought home to me forcibly, for the first time, just what a terrible situation we were in; as far as I could see there did not seem to be any solution. I could not even imagine what future there could be for me—or for any of us—virtually penniless, our hearts constricted with anguish, our minds constantly bewildered by strange sights and sounds, our bodies racked with unaccustomed heat and lack of food, longing for a breath of thin clear mountain air; all of us, pitchforked into an unknown world, a strange century and each of us as vulnerable and ill-equipped for our new situation as a newborn babe.

As I tossed around in the dark, I had never felt so alone and gripped by despair. The faces of some of the Tibetans who had crowded round us when we arrived came into my mind as I tried mentally to recognize someone who might have known my parents or who came from Drekung area—a trader who might have visited our village or someone from one of the monasteries round Bhakar who could give me news of my home, perhaps even to tell me my parents had escaped and were even now in this camp or one of the other camps receiving refugees along the Indian border.

With such thoughts for company, the night seemed endless, I longed for dawn. My impatient longing reminded me of New Year's Eve at home when all Tibetan children lie awake looking forward to the dawn of Losar morning when they will find their New Year gifts of clothes and presents; only now I longed for dawn so that I could hope to find someone with news of my parents or even—and I trembled with excitement at the thought —my parents themselves!

In an effort to distract my thoughts from alternate worry and wishful thinking, I began to stare at the diminishing light of the kerosene lamp at my end of the hut. I wondered why it was left on all night. It seemed to me to be very dangerous— bamboo is very dry and highly inflammable, in those crowded conditions the lamp could easily be knocked over by a tossing sleeper. I looked about me at the dim bundles of people on the bamboo shelves; they were now mostly silent, occasionally flapping a hand against the tireless mosquitoes. My uncle and brother were sound asleep, untroubled evidently by such anxious thoughts as tormented me. Most of the mosquitoes seemed to be clouding round the lamp and it occurred to me that perhaps it was left alight for just such a purpose, to attract as many mosquitoes as possible away from the sleeping Tibetans.

My thin blanket was poor protection against the lumps and sharpness of the shelf and finally, about four o'clock in the morning, I got up to take off the shredded remains of my chuba, rolled it into some semblance of a mattress, curled up and slowly drifted off into a sleep full of memories of home.

15

THE DOOR TO A NEW WORLD

ALMOST immediately it seemed to be morning and time to get up. The first thing to be done was to report to the camp officer. When we reached his office I was delighted to see my teacher, whom I had last seen at Norbulingka. We exchanged greetings and although he had been very strict with me at school in Lhasa, he seemed very pleased to see me now and told me at once that I would still be his pupil, he would arrange lessons for me in camp. I received this news with rather mixed feelings, but in any case he was transferred from Missamari before the lessons could be organized.

The camp officer told my uncle we were to move to the staff quarters and he was to be the Tibetan camp leader. We were shown two bamboo houses containing the Indian staff rooms and an office for my uncle which was also his bedroom. My brother, our cook and I were allotted a good-sized room in the second house which we shared with other Tibetan members of the camp staff.

Missamari was strictly a transit camp and there was a constant flow of Tibetans passing through. With the help and co-operation of Pandit Nehru's government, settlement schemes and roadworks were being arranged by His Holiness the Dalai Lama and other Tibetan leaders already in Dharamsala. As soon as Tibetans arrived in Missamari they registered their names and occupations and in most cases, if they were fit enough, they were soon transferred to the newly forming centres or road camps.

But the Tibetans are a mountain people and for many of them the heat and heavy atmosphere of the plains proved too much; their resistance was already almost gone from the privations of their journey. There were several deaths almost every day, from heat stroke, starvation and, later on, tuberculosis.

The Indians did what they could to help, and indeed they were extremely generous when one remembers their own problems of hunger and housing for their huge population. The sudden influx of refugees posed a great problem, especially during the first few months, when each bamboo longhouse was immediately filled to overflowing as soon as it was completed. At that time and for some time to come the Indians shouldered the burden of assisting us alone; there was no other help or organization as the world in general was unaware of the Tibetans' plight and they were not officially included in any world refugee assistance.

The Indian Government proposed to lease a tract of forest in Mysore State to be cleared for agriculture and settled by 3,000 refugees. Many people, especially the farmers, put their names on the register for this scheme and prepared to wait in Missamari until the scheme could be got under way.

Other Tibetans knew of relatives or friends already arrived and settled in the rapidly building Tibetan communities further west, in Mussoorie, Darjeeling, Simla and other places. Newly arrived lamas were mostly transferred to Dalhousie, where there was a growing lama community.

For many, the Indians provided work building roads in the Himalayas.

So, one way and another, there was a constant stream of Tibetans flowing through Missamari. But in all the thousands who passed through during the months I was there, I never saw a familiar face or heard a word about my parents.

After we had seen the camp officer and arranged our accommodation, we joined the very long queue of people waiting for a clothing issue. Everyone was given one grey cotton shirt and a pair of grey cotton trousers. They were all identical so we all

L

looked as though we were in uniform! Then we joined the food queue. We were given rice, dahl, flour, salt, sugar, tea, powdered milk, khado (a kind of pumpkin) and meat once a fortnight. In the beginning the quantities were quite lavish, but as the camp became more and more overcrowded, the quantities diminished as the supplies had to be spread ever more sparingly to give everyone a little.

On arrival we were all given a mug and a plate each and every family or group a large aluminium cooking pot and a tea kettle. We also received a ration of firewood for cooking, but this was not enough; we supplemented it with driftwood from the nearby river. There was also a forest at the edge of the plain, but we were not allowed to chop wood from the trees, only to gather any that had fallen naturally.

The river flowed through a small wood at the back of the camp. Many people constantly drenched themselves in the water to try and cool off a little from the searing heat of the plain. Splashing about in the river was one of my favourite occupations, but sometimes even the water of the river became too hot for us to bathe in it! Having only one set of clothes presented problems too. I tried to choose a quiet time, when there were not many others at the river, usually in the intensified heat of the afternoon sun, wash my clothes quickly whilst I stood waist deep in the river, then lay them on the bank and hide in the woods until they were dry. Fortunately in that terrible heat they did not take very long to dry!

Many Tibetans, accustomed to cool mountain air, suffered severely from the heat—I have heard them saying that an egg could be boiled in the sand—but for some reason I was not particularly uncomfortable; perhaps because the element ruling the year of my birth was fire! But most people found it difficult to acclimatize, many of them sweltered and died every day and many more were sick for a very long time. There was a hospital in the camp, consisting of three bamboo longhouses which were always full. There was no room for anyone who was not really seriously ill. The dangerously ill and dying were taken to a hospital in Tezpur, about 50 miles away. Very few of these ever returned to the camp; most of them were too desperately ill to recover.

There was also a small bamboo shelter where everyone who was still able to walk at all went for daily treatment. Here there was also an issue of vitamin tablets. There was always a very long queue of people waiting and for the first month I joined the queue to receive treatment for all the running sores on my legs and feet, a legacy from the multitude of leech bites on my journey.

The Indians were very good to us at this time. There were very few nurses and doctors to cope with the multitude of sick and they must often have been exhausted by the interminable queues of genuinely ill patients and depressed by the inadequacy of the means at their disposal in their great-hearted efforts to help us.

All too soon after we arrived in camp my uncle bought me a slate and a piece of chalk and found someone who could teach me English. My teacher was a Tibetan man who knew only a very little English, but still nobody else knew any at all and in the country of the blind the one-eyed man is king!

He began with A.B.C. and by the end of the second day I could write and say the alphabet by heart. Then he went on to teach me small unrelated words like ant, boy, cat. My lessons started at nine in the morning and finished at ten, then my uncle would call me to sit beside him and continue my studies. I sat cross legged on the ground staring at the letters on my slate and missing my trips to the river. It seemed it would never be *bara bachi*, which is Hindi for twelve o'clock, but which to the Tibetans was Hindi for lunch time! Then at last my uncle would say I might go and have my lunch. For all I wanted to rush off I sometimes found my legs had gone to sleep after sitting cross-legged for so long and it was a minute or two before I could hurry away. Although *bara bachi* was relief as well as lunch time for me, I was never successful in my after-lunch attempts to go off and play with some of the new friends I had made in camp. My uncle would soon find me and back I would be sitting beside him poring over my slate. I was very thankful when my teacher was transferred to another camp after about a month and my uncle could not find anyone else to teach me. I had not learnt very much, but I could write the alphabet and say "What is your name?" in English!

It was not long before my uncle was sent to Gangtok, the capital of Ladakh, to be leader of the Tibetan camp there. Just before he left, he told me he had included my name in a list of twenty boys selected to go to study in Denmark on a scheme to be run by a private Danish committee. He said it would not be more than two weeks before we left for Denmark and I was to wait in the camp with my brother.

My brother and I went down to the bus station to see him off. I was very sad to find that our cook was going to Gangtok with him. Ever since I first arrived in Lhasa to live with my uncle, the cook had taken great care of me and I liked him very much. As he was leaving he gave me a rupee, saying he had very little money but he hoped the rupee would buy me a pencil to help me with my studies. I promised him I would spend it only on a pencil and not on anything to play with. They climbed into the truck which served the camp as a bus, we said good-bye and the truck rolled down the road until it disappeared into the forest at the edge of the camp. I stood there staring after the truck, tears streaming down my face until my brother tapped me on the shoulder and told me briskly that we must go back to the camp.

I never saw the cook again. Three years later my uncle wrote to tell me he had been killed in an avalanche which swamped a camp in Kulu Menali. I was heart-broken by this news. During my stay with my uncle this man had been my dearest and kindest friend; I always went to him with all my trouble. On our journey across the Himalayas, I doubt if I would have managed to arrive in Missamari safely had it not been for his constant help and care for me. It seemed terrible that he should have survived so many hazards, often literally carving a way for us through the jungle, leading us to safety with his courage and resourcefulness, always taking the first and most dangerous steps forward, only to die so sadly soon after reaching India.

After my uncle left camp, I had much more free time. Some weeks before, I had found a bicycle in the office. I noticed that it was never used so on the rare occasions when I could escape my uncle's vigilance I had secretly started to teach myself to ride it. Now with my uncle gone, I had much more time to practise. I was rather small and the bicycle was quite big; the saddle was about level with my shoulder, but with a little practice every day I soon learnt to ride it by standing on the pedals with my right leg under the cross bar.

This accomplishment came in very useful because the camp officers decided to appoint me the camp postman at a salary of 50 NPs a day (about 6d. at that time). At first I felt rather embarrassed by this offer, I was very shy and afraid that this 'job' would draw attention to myself, but finally I agreed to try it.

The next morning I collected the bag of letters and stamp money from the camp officer, who explained to me that the post office was about 4 miles away. I rode off on the bicycle and found the post office quite easily, but since I had no idea how to handle the letters or buy the stamps I waited about watching the other postmen for a while to learn how to do it as professionally as possible. When I felt I had seen enough I took my turn at handing in the letters and bought the stamps. The camp officer had taught me how to count the Indian money so I had no difficulty with the change. I collected the letters to be delivered to the camp and on my return the camp officer called the names of the addressees over the camp loudspeaker so that the people could call for them.

There was a railway station at the back of the post office and I could seldom resist going to watch the trains before setting off back to camp with the mail. It was not a very big station, now I come to think of it, in comparison with many other railway stations I have since seen, but at that time I thought it was very big, quite large enough for me to fear I might lose my way if I ventured too far. But mechanical things such as trains and other modern transport aroused great interest in me and I had longed to see all these things ever since my mother had first told me about them. No matter how crowded and noisy the station I could never resist the lure of the train's whistle.

I used to think how lucky I was to have the job of postman, it allowed me to see so many new and interesting things. The other Tibetans were not allowed out of camp except on Mondays and Wednesdays when it was market day; few of them had any money to shop at the market but they went there anyway when they had the chance, to gaze, like me, with interest and amazement at the strange new world they had fled to. As postman I was able to see new things every day. Sometimes I used to go to the military camp, which also contained the airport where we had landed. I spent fascinated hours watching the soldiers marching and training, doing P.T. and playing basket ball. I enjoyed watching basket ball particularly, it is a game played quite a lot in Tibet. Sometimes I wished I could be a soldier and join the basket ball team, and have a smart uniform and march about. Luckily I was unable to do this because I am sure I would not have enjoyed it for very long!

About a fortnight after I had become the postman, the camp loud speaker broke down and I had to deliver all the letters personally to each hut and give out any messages or camp announcements. I did not like this new part of my job at all. Giving out the messages and camp announcements was the worst. By now there were 160 long bamboo houses. In each house I must shout out the message twice, once in the upper end of the 60-foot-long room and again at the lower end. It was not only crammed to bursting with people chattering and reminiscing and condoling with each other, but the majority of them were country people speaking a variety of dialects who could not understand my Central Tibetan speech. In some of the houses they were very good, listening attentively and helping me to make myself understood, even inviting me to join them for a meal. But in many of the other houses the people regarded my arrival as a cue for their entertainment. They would make me repeat the message again and again, long after they had understood, mocking my accent, pretending they couldn't hear me and generally making fun of me. I was very pleased when the loud speaker was repaired and I no longer had to call in at the houses every day but only occasionally to announce a special house-cleaning programme in preparation for an important visit or inspection or some such thing.

I was now in the camp alone, my brother had left for Dalhousie where he was to study at a newly opened handicraft centre. Before he left he told me to study hard in Denmark but I was beginning to wonder if I would ever get there; it was over a month since my uncle had left for Gangtok and I had heard nothing more about going to Denmark.

I had made friends with two other boys my uncle had listed for Denmark and they too were now in the camp on their own, waiting to hear when we were to leave for our studies; their parents had been transferred to more permanent camps. Now the cook and my brother had left I had our room to myself so I invited my two friends to share it. We had plenty to do; the camp officer had detailed Sonam and Tsering to collect firewood, which kept them busy whilst I went to the post office.

Soon I was given the additional task of shopping for the Indian staff and some of the Tibetans who were able to supplement their rations.

Most of the Tibetans had escaped from Tibet by different, less tortuous routes than the one we had taken and had been able to bring with them a varying amount of possessions, which they sold piece by piece for money for necessities. Some had even started out with a fair proportion of their cattle but had had to sell them on the way. In some instances they had been told that their heavy-coated cattle, especially yak, would not survive in the Indian climate. On hearing this they had been glad to part with them for sometimes less than one rupee a head only to find later in India that their cattle would have thrived. Many too had been persuaded to part with their sheep-skins and warm clothing for a mere song on the pretext that the Indian climate would be far too hot for such clothing. Alas, when they eventually found themselves in the winter hills of Simla and Mussoorie, many were the times when they longed for the warmth of their sheepskins and woollens sold for a few pence to their cunning informants!

On Mondays I went to a small local market about 5 miles away and on Thursdays to a bigger one 8 miles away returning with my bicycle laden with vegetables, eggs and meat.

One Thursday after cycling some way along the main road I decided to turn off down a small path which I knew was a short cut leading eventually to the market. As I was riding gaily along the front wheel of the bicycle fell off, the prongs either side of the hub went straight into the ground and stuck there throwing me forward into the mud. When I stood up I saw that the wheel had rolled several yards away but the bicycle was still standing upright. I was very worried, I had no idea how to repair the bike and even if I had, I had no tools. I felt quite helpless. I took the wheel and tried ineffectually to put it on, but I could not see where it had really come off or what to fix it to. I was beginning to despair when fortunately an Indian villager came along on a bicycle laden with oranges for the market. He was one of the most sensible and kind-hearted men I have ever met in India. He could see at once what was the matter and immediately dismounted and set about helping me to fix my wheel. He explained that the nuts holding the wheel had fallen off. By great good fortune he not only had a tool case but he also had some nuts. He mended my bicycle very nicely and would not take a penny for it. I was very grateful and thanked him very much.

I usually managed to get back from the market in time to join Sonam and Tsering for our evening chore of fetching the cookhouse water from the river which was about a mile away at the back of the camp. We all enjoyed the trip down to the river when our big square petrol tins were empty. Sonam would dance all the way whilst Tsering and I beat time on our empty tins with sticks; but coming back was different! We had our water-filled tins to carry on our backs, they were very heavy but we usually passed the time planning a new dance for Sonam to try next time.

I used to get very hungry and watched for a chance to creep

into the kitchen, which was rather dark, and take an egg, pierce it with a pin, suck it and return the empty shell to the basket quickly! I once emptied an egg, filled it with milky tea then stuck the shell together. Cook was mystified . . . he thought the egg was bad!

When I first started doing the marketing I was still rather unused to handling money and inclined to be rather careless with it. I was once given five rupees to buy eggs. I simply put

Losing a wheel

the note loosely in the wire basket of my bicycle. Not surprisingly I had not cycled very far before it blew away! I am afraid that when I had to explain why I had not bought the eggs, I said that a big Indian had taken the note from me (I was very small!). As it was a Tibetan who had given me the money I was believed because some Indians did this sort of thing—particularly 'buying' jewellery from the Tibetans then quickly disappearing with it in the bazaar crowd without paying for it, leaving the Tibetan standing bereft, sadder and wiser.

As my uncle was leaving he had given me twenty rupees. I still had no shoes so the first time I went to market I decided I would buy some with this money. This was really my first experience of buying anything for myself (unless I count the five peanuts I bought on the ship!) and after a good deal of consideration I paid fifteen rupees for quite a nice looking pair of shoes which the shopkeeper promised me were real leather. A week later the monsoon arrived and in the first rain the shoes disintegrated completely . . . they were made of cardboard! So I was barefoot again and remained so until I eventually left for Denmark many months later when I was issued with an enormous pair of wellingtons for the journey.

But at this time there was still no news of leaving for Denmark and I began to think I was going to stay in this camp forever! A considerable number of Tibetans had already been dispersed to other camps and others were leaving almost every day. For those still remaining the Tibetan camp leader had set up a small school in three of the bamboo longhouses which were now empty. Two of these were adjacent but the third was some distance away. This separate one was for beginners and anyone who wished to do so could attend the classes. Many of the older Tibetans who had never learnt to read or write took the opportunity to join this Class I to have reading and writing instruction.

Class II was for those who already had a little knowledge of elementary Tibetan letters and Class III was 'Advanced'. Sonam, Tsering and I had all been to school in Tibet and attended Class III.

Classes were held from 9 a.m. to 11.30 a.m. and 2 p.m. till 3 p.m. Everyone was welcome to join and the classes were packed at every session with adults and children.

Class I, the alphabet class, was taught by students from Class III, four of whom took it in turns to teach the beginners. Classes II and III were taught by laymen who had been educated in private schools in Lhasa.

Sonam and I found a huge empty petrol container which we cleaned and polished until it shone before we suspended it from a pole. This was our school bell! We clubbed it mightily with thick sticks and the harsh notes rang out all over the camp.

There was also a Tibetan 'camp interpreter' who had been

educated in Darjeeling. He spoke both Hindi and English very well and organized evening classes for these languages and so my friends and I began to learn English.

About this time a school was being started in Mussoorie by Mr and Mrs Taring and twenty-five of the children still remaining in our camp were transferred to it.

Gradually the rest of the people began to move on until finally there were only some hospital patients too ill to be moved and we boys, now ten of us, still waiting to go to Denmark.

We had the whole camp to ourselves for about a fortnight, then the Indian Special Officer and the Tibetan camp leader decided it would be best for us to be sent to Mussoorie and to wait there for our papers to come through for our long awaited journey to Denmark. The hospital patients were also transferred, to Tezpur, and Missamari camp closed down.

Before we left the ten of us received a letter from our Tibetan Bureau in Delhi, authorizing our admission as temporary pupils to the new Mussoorie school, and we set off by train. After twenty-four hours we arrived in Dehra Dun and took the bus that follows the winding road for 7,000 feet to reach Mussoorie, strung like a necklace round the crest of the wooded mountain and only 40 miles, as the crow flies, from Tibet, but for us now as out of reach as the furthest planet.

When we arrived at the school we found about 100 boys and girls already installed. It was evening. We were put into one of the many empty houses left by the British; we were very tired and soon asleep.

The following day we had tests in Tibetan, English and Hindi. I was glad I had taken the opportunity to attend the evening classes in Missamari; I had learnt quite a lot of English phrases and a smattering of Hindi. We had all worked hard at our English and thought we had learnt quite a lot, but in the oral examination in Mussoorie the teacher was bewildered by our pronunciation. He admitted that we certainly seemed to know a lot of English phrases but he had no idea what we were talking about because he could not understand our accents! We were very crestfallen! However, we were assigned to various classes.

Life in Mussoorie was very different from the quiet secluded life in Bhakar and Tsela Dzong, even from the simple camp life of Assam. At first, as with meeting people in any place, I felt I was left alone in a vast impersonal stadium hemmed in by noise and crowds who wanted nothing to do with me. I still had very little idea how to mix with people and forward friendships, the constant surge of new faces and group activities made my head buzz and my spirit tremble. I ached for some stillness and the quiet security of my home.

Early every morning we went down to the gravel football pitch to do P.T. I still had no shoes and only my cotton shirt and trousers. After the extreme heat of Assam the cold high mountain air was very chilly! The gravel playground was covered with small sharp stones which I found very painful for my bare feet, hardened though they were, and the cold was a great discomfort.

After we had been in Mussoorie for almost three months we were told at last that we were to be given travel documents and could leave for Denmark. Almost exactly one year after my uncle had told me he had included my name on the list of candidates and I would be leaving in a fortnight!

We were all instructed to go down to the library bazaar to have our photographs taken for our passports. I was in transports of excitement. But the day before we were to do this, I fell heavily in the playground and cut my knee wide open. Blood poured from the gash, great lumps of red flesh, like butcher's meat, stuck out from the exposed bone of my knee cap. I managed to hobble to our house without being seen and flooded my knee with water in an effort to staunch the blood. Then I took a cloth and bound it tightly round my leg, still trying to stop it bleeding. I was panic-stricken by the thought that perhaps I would not now be able to go to Denmark after looking forward to it and waiting all this time.

I lay down on my bed in despair with my knee throbbing like a beating drum, wondering how in the world I was going to manage the three mile walk to the bazaar in the morning to have my passport picture taken.

I spent a very restless night tormented both by the pain and the anxiety of how to walk to the bazaar. Already my knee was so painful and swollen that I could hardly bear to put it to the ground and I certainly did not think I would be able to walk at all in the morning.

At last the sky began to show the first pale signs of dawn. I crawled out of bed, as I put my foot gingerly to the ground I nearly screamed with pain, biting my tongue in an effort to be quiet and not disturb the others. I decided that if I was going to manage the 3 miles to the bazaar I had better start at once; a slow, very slow excruciating hobble was the best I could achieve and at this snail's pace it would take me hours. Every house in Mussoorie stands on a steep slope of the mountain side and ours was no exception. I inched my way to the front door and started off down the sharply inclined path that led to the road by the school. The sun was still tucked behind the mountains and the morning air was bitter but I was sweating with pain and the concentration of trying to move forward. By the time I reached the road, less than 100 yards from the house, the snows that capped the peaks of Nanda Devi were turning from pink to gold in the rising sun. I rested against a tree for a few moments and saw that my knee must have started to bleed again. The cloth I had wound round it the night before was saturated and the blood was beginning to trickle down my leg. I set off again up the steep hill that runs by the side of the school; dot and carry, dot and carry, slowly I hobbled past the football pitch. By now the pain was almost unendurable and I began to realize despairingly that it was impossible to walk to the bazaar. I crawled on until I reached a bank low enough to sit on by the side of the road. I was too heart-broken even to cry, I just sat there overwhelmed with hopelessness.

I don't know how long I had been sitting there when I suddenly saw Mr Taring come out of his office and walk across the playground towards me. I could not believe it! He was coming up to me! I tried to get to my feet but it was impossible.

He stood in front of me, puzzled and concerned to know why I was sitting looking so dejectedly by the side of the road so early in the morning, then he noticed my bandaged swollen knee and at once his face flooded with sympathy and understanding. Without more ado he gave me three rupees and told me to take a rickshaw to the bazaar to have my passport picture taken. I thought I would burst with gratitude and relief. I shall never forget this kindness for as long as I live; his quick understanding and generosity at that moment opened the door to the new world of study and experience that I had thought, a moment before, had slammed in my face.

So I went to the bazaar in a rickshaw, I got my passport, my knee was treated and began to heal. I got my first pair of 'shoes' for nearly a year, an enormous pair of old wellington boots from the refugee clothing supplies. And I left for Denmark and my first encounter with the Yellowheads—the Tibetan for Europeans.